THE *Spiritual* REBELLION

RECLAIMING UNITY, LOVE, AND SACRED SOVEREIGNTY

*Everyone knows there must be a change in the world
It begins with the heart*

LINDA DILLON

The Spiritual Rebellion
Reclaiming Love, Light and Sacred Sovereignty

By Linda Dillon

© 2026 by Linda Dillon

Published by Council of Love, Inc.

All Rights Reserved

This book contains copyrighted material protected under International and Federal Copyright Laws and Treaties.

Additional study materials for this book are available at lindadillonauthor.com

Dedication

To the Girls—my wonderful powerful Soul Sisters, creative and nurturing—who walk though the dark nights of the soul, and turn your faces to the sun. To the women seen and unseen, present and gone ahead, who create a better world every day—one heart at a time. To all those who embrace the girl within, who remember how to laugh and cry and giggle.

Acknowledgment

With deepest gratitude and infinite Love, I offer thanks to all those who have walked, wept, laughed, and soared with me in this Spiritual Rebellion of a journey into Unity.

To the Divine Mother, Archangels, Ascended Masters, Star Family, and the entire Council of Love—thank you for your unwavering presence, your loving nudges, your sacred teachings, and your constant companionship. This book is born of guidance and grace.

To my family and loved ones, who have held space for my mission with understanding and patience, thank you for your support, your love, and your faith in my path.

To the Council of Love community, the healers, teachers, pathfinders, and loveholders who have joined me in the co-creation of Nova Earth—your dedication, wisdom, and lived example of Unity Consciousness are an inspiration. You are the heartbeat of this work.

To my editorial collaborators, friends who offered insights and encouragement behind the scenes, thank you for helping shape this book with care and clarity.

To my partner, editor and graphic designer thank you for your never-ending support, inspiration, encouragement and patience.

To my beloved students and clients, who trusted me with their hearts and healing—you are sacred mirrors of courage and transformation. Your willingness to say yes to your soul's evolution is part of what makes this world new.

And finally, to Gaia, our planetary archangel, for cradling us in her embrace and modeling the very essence of sacred unity.

May this book serve as a lantern, a song, a gentle reminder of who we are and what we are here to become—together.

Thank you—from my heart to yours, all my love.

Preface

The Purpose of This Book

Our world is on fire, chaos is rampant. The political, social and structural upheaval is global. The dark emotions of hatred, domination and greed are on the surface of humanity. So many of us are left feeling disillusioned, weary and wounded at every level.

Access to communication has never been more available yet there is an epidemic of loneliness, a longing for meaningful connection, and an overwhelming sense of alienation. People are hungry for new pathways of being that do not involve judgment, fear, abuse and blame.

And there is a way—a path forward forged by heaven and designed for humanity. A new grid for humanity of kindness, inclusiveness, harmony and peace. A path that eliminates judgment, hostility and rampant ego. A path that leads us back to our hearts and our innate knowing of love.

We are not lost. This collective and personal desire, demand for connection and community is our catalyst to embracing new pathways and patterns of engagement. And the purpose of this book is to conjoin with you in forging those pathways—together, heart to heart to heart.

As channel for the Council of Love, I humbly offer to guide you through a process that results in understanding the road ahead—the anchoring of new patterns, fresh paradigms of what it means to be human. To walk with you, hand in hand, heart to heart from chaos to peace, from exclusion to expansion. To awaken and anchor within your life the knowing that already rests within, that is expressing in this desire to exit and eliminate judgment, division and conflict.

I am a pacifist at heart. War, conflict, and cruelty are aberrations. They have no place in our sacred selves, our communities or upon Gaia. Patterns of behavior that create divisions of I'm right and you're wrong, I know the real story—you're stupid and naive have no place—they don't grow corn. Our bodies, minds and souls are sick of the us/them paradigm. It's time to shift.

I am passionate about what I do—as a channel, teacher, healer and woman. I care deeply about our collective journey upon Gaia—about what we are co-creating right here, right now—as the COL puts it on planet, in from.

That is the purpose of this book—to heal the wounds of this war of separation and to together claim and anchor a world that works for everyone. A world based on what the COL calls the Keys to Heaven: Love, trust, forgiveness—unity, connectedness and balance.

Every time I write a book, it becomes far more than a project of words—it is an adventure of spirit. I sit with the Council of Love in the stillness and ask: How can I help? What would you have me share? I don't write simply to inspire, though I hope there's plenty of that. I write as a bridge for those who are yearning. I write to midwife change. I write for you—if you are searching for your Why, your How, your place in this world of upheaval and possibility.

One morning, in the quiet pre-dawn hours, I asked Archangel Gabrielle: "Why a Spiritual Rebellion to Unity? Why now?" Her answer was unmistakable:

> "Greetings, I am Gabrielle, Lily of Love, Trumpet of Truth. We write the opus of Unity, this manifesto of freedom. And by 'we' I mean not only you and I, child, but the Unified Field of One… The new paradigm of humanity is Unity. You have entered a new realm of existence; there will be moments when this landscape feels foreign, unknown, even unknowable. Yet, you are accompanied through every step. That is why we write this opus—because we love you and because it is time."

Those words did not simply echo—they anchored me. This isn't just my work. It is our work. This isn't a solo voice. It is the chorus of the Unified Field of One—Mother, Father, One, the archangels and ascended masters, our star family, the kingdoms of Earth and stars.

Our work is not only to inspire but to catalyze real change—a way for you to seek answers to your Why and How. These pages offer refined attunements to connect and guide you in your search for insight and answers, to shift perspectives into a more profound experience of joy and fulfillment. You are not only worthy of Love but designed to expand and evolve in the knowingness of that Love. I know this—it is my life's work; it's the core of everything I do and share.

My path of service is not only to explain what is, not only to provide a glimpse of what lies ahead, but to share the roadmap—to install the GPS—and explain how to utilize it! This pathfinder role has been granted to me by the Divine Mother, and it forms the foundation of my work with the Council of Love (COL). Together, we peer into the ever-expanding essence of One, sharing what lies beyond the horizon.

We are not alone in this unfolding. We are being supported, inspired, and loved every step of the way.

As Gabrielle once reminded us:

> "God is a being beyond comprehension to most, even to those who have spent eons in God's embrace… The Universe is not static; it is a living, breathing force, ever-changing and expanding in awareness."

Unity is not an abstract ideal. It is a remembering, and

a choice. It is the fundamental truth that we belong—to each other, to Gaia, to Love itself.

And if you are reading these words, know this: You are already joined the Spiritual Rebellion. Unity is already at work within you.

What This Book Offers

This book is not another list of things to do. It is not here to hurry you or add to your burdens.

It is here to be your companion. To meet you where you are. To walk beside you. To gently remind you of what you already know.

Within these pages you will find:

- Definitions and teachings that give language to what your heart already senses.
- Channeled messages that awaken your knowing and expand your remembering.
- Personal reflections — not to center my story, but to walk alongside yours.
- The Divine Mother's Questions — sacred invitations to go deeper, not outward, but inward.

And through it all, the loving presence of the Council of Love.

Please don't rush. Let each chapter, each section, settle like morning mist—soft, real, alive. This book is an offering. A mirror. A doorway.

Take your time with this book. After reading a chapter or two, pause to let it sink in, allowing the energy to settle within you. This process isn't meant to be rushed but savored. This is a journey we take together, led by the guidance and love of the Council of Love.

The Why of this work is simple: to prepare you, to ignite you, to remind you of the thrill and beauty of walking in Unity Consciousness on Nova Earth.

We are ready. You are ready.

Contents

The Purpose of This Book v

    What This Book Offers..ix

Chapter One - The Spiritual Rebellion 1

    The Invitation to Unity 3

    Saying Yes to Unity...4

    Walking in Union 5

    The Awakening 5

    Realizing Unity 6

    A Deeper Purpose 7

    The Progression: A Divine Unfolding 9

    The Conjunction: A Divine Reset 10

    Cracks in the Old Paradigm..................................11

    Divine Radiance: A Living Grace 12

    Harmonizing: The Dance of Becoming.................13

    Sacred Love and Unity: The Next Horizon..........14

    The Long Arc of Preparation................................15

    You Are Ready 15

Chapter Two - What is Unity 17

    The Challenge of Becoming.................................20

The Universal Drive 21

The Experience of Unity 22

Unity as the Third Rail 24

Beyond Time 24

The Mother's Question 26

Chapter Three - Humanity's Journey to Unity 28

The Soil of Change 28

From Cultural Change to Civic
Engagement to Political Evolution 30

Cultural Change: The Seed of
Transformation 31

Civic Engagement: Transforming
Culture into Action 32

Political Change: Embodying New
Values in Law 34

The Interplay Between Cultural, Civic, and
Political Change 35

The Role of Individuals in the
Cycle of Change 36

Harmonizing with Evolution 37

From Cultural Change to Civic Action to Political
Evolution—The Influence of Universal Law 38

The Foundation of Universal Law 39

Cultural Change: Awakening to
Universal Truths 39

Civic Engagement: Living the Laws of Love 40

Political Change: Transforming Structures with Universal Principles 41

The Interconnected Dance of Change 42

Harmonizing with Universal Law 44

Yes, It's Personal 45

The Mother's Question 46

Chapter Four - Where Are We? 47

Seeing with New Eyes 48

The Signs of Change 49

Personal Reflection: Recognizing Divine Patterns .. 50

The Essence of Divine Sequencing 51

Humanity's Awakening 52

Gaia's Voice: A Call to Co-Create 55

Personal Reflection: Morning Light 56

A Vision of Unity 58

Core Elements of Unity 60

Navigating the Journey of Unity 60

The New Normal as a Journey of Fabulous Unshackled Neutrality 62

Embracing the Path of Transformation 63

Chapter Five - The Foundation of Enduring Principles 64

A Question to the Council 64

The 13th Octave: A Divine Gift of Unity 66

The New Grid of Humanity 69

Universal Law: An Invitation to Live by Love 70

Sanat Kumara's Invitation 71

The Essence of Universal Law 72

A Foundation of Timeless Guidance 73

Conscious Creation 74

Sacred Creation: Our Gift and Calling 74

The Creation Formula: A Sacred Overview............75

Step 1: Intention...76

Step 2: Stillpoint...77

Step 3: Action...78

Embrace Joy and Gratitude 79

A Message from The Divine Mother:
I Have Called You 80

Conclusion: Foundation of Enduring Principles 81

Personal Reflection...82

The Mother's Question..84

Chapter Six - Sacred Love 87

The Essence of Sacred Love 87

The Ongoing Journey 89

All Love Is Sacred 91

Knowing Your Sacred Self 92

Personal Reflection...93

Heartbreak as Portal...94

The Awakening 97

Meditation: Embracing Sacred Love 99

Chapter Seven - Embracing Sacred Union 102

How Sacred Union Fits the Larger Sequencing........104

Sacred Union: The Expression of Sacred Love 105

The Layers of Sacred Union..107

Sacred Partnership: A Unique
Expression of Sacred Union 108

What does Sacred Love mean to you?.......................111

Personal Reflection: My Journey of Sacred Union..113

The Mother's Question...116

Chapter Eight - The Art of Heart Communication ... 118

Language as Living Energy...121

The Universal Language of the Heart........................122

The Language of Channeling.......................................122

The Unspoken Language of Understanding 124

Star Family Language...125

1. Perro (pair-o)..126

2. Paca (pack-a) 127

3. Badu (baa-too)...127

4. Saedor (say-door) 127

Divine Neutrality...128

A Message from Galea, Communications
Officer, UFOG..129

Practicing Saedor: A Heart
Communication Activation.............................130

Speaking from the Waves of Love.............................132

Shifting to Heart Communication.............................134

Returning to Divine Neutrality.................................137

The How To's of Heart Communication....................138

Practicing Heart Speaking & Heart Listening..........140

The Mother's Question..144

Chapter Nine - The Framework of Unity Consciousness..146

Divine Authority..148

Divine Authority: A Loving Invitation
from the Mother 150

Harmonizing with Divine Radiance.........................152

Personal Reflection: Harmonizing
with Divine Radiance..154

Living Harmonization: The Mother's Invitation 155

The Mother's Question:..158

Divine Knowing...158

Divine Neutrality...163

A Misunderstood Teaching 164

Anchoring Divine Neutrality 164

Why is Divine Neutrality so challenging?................165

The Good News: Nova Earth's
Blueprint Already Exists 166

How do we Embody Divine Neutrality? 167

The Mother's Question & Sacred Assignment 169

Conclusion 170

Chapter Ten- The Nova Gaian Qualities 171

Who (or What) is Nova Gaian? 172

But who or what is a Nova Gaian? 173

Vulnerability: The Keystone Quality 176

Motivation: Understanding our Inner Drives 181

Passion & Intimacy: Interwoven Threads
of Sacred Union 184

Refined Balance: Aligning Ready,
Willing & Able 186

Willing Surrender 187

Practicing Discernment: Eliminating
Doubt, Anchoring Trust 189

Living the Heart of Divine Neutrality 192

Practicing Divine Neutrality: The Nova Gaian
Stance 194

How Do We Live This? 195

What do you do? 196

Divine Neutrality as Sacred Action 196

The Mother's Question 198

Chapter Eleven - The Spiritual Rebellion;
The Call to Action 199

    Sacred Action: Your Love in Motion 211

    Flourish & Nourish 212

    Examples of Flourish & Nourish in Action 213

    Expand & Elevate 214

    Reflect 214

    Examples of Expansion & Elevation in Action 214

    Passion & Devotion 215

    Examples of Passion & Devotion in Action 215

    The Sacred Invitation 216

    From Spark to Flame 217

    From Grassroots to Great Change:
    The Power of Unified Action 220

    Personal Reflection 222

    More Help from the Divine Mother 225

    The Speed of Love 226

    Closing Thoughts: Join The Spiritual Rebellion 227

    The Call to Action 229

Chapter One

The Spiritual Rebellion

The Spiritual Rebellion declares there is another way—a pathway grounded in Unity, not separation and discord; in Love, not hatred and conflict; in connection, not arrogance or ego. It is not about turning away, but turning toward—toward our sacred selves, toward solutions, patterns, and behaviors that are creative and inclusive rather than destructive. It is about choosing to embrace our fellow humans rather than ignoring collective pain.

This rebellion is not abstract or purely esoteric—it is deeply rooted in the heart. It's about anchoring in our knowing—a knowing that has always lived within us—and choosing to act from that place. It is the conscious decision to say there is another way and to live that truth in form. It is the courage to create what the heart yearns for without harming others. It is allowing inspiration to blossom into intention, and intention into action—propelling you, and through you, the collective—into co-creating a world that works for everyone.

2

Effective rebellions are never solitary. They arise from collective movement—shared values, shared dreams, shared acts of daring. The Spiritual Rebellion is a collective awakening, an uprising that leads to a fundamental paradigm shift in how we live, govern, and grow as societies, cultures, and as a planet. It is not defined by what we oppose, but by what we stand for. It is the sacred expression of our mission on Earth—our covenant with each other and with the Divine.

For years, the Council of Love has addressed us as Warriors of Love, Warriors of Peace, Bravehearts, and Champions of Change. These have not been idle salutations—they have been the quiet heralding of our roles in this great rebellion long before it was named. What may have appeared as a slow simmer beneath the chaos has in truth been a Divine orchestration—awaiting this exact moment.

When I asked the Divine Mother why She chose a title that some might find provocative or even confrontational, She replied:

> "Dearhearts, Angels of Change, I choose this title because it embodies action. It speaks to the decision to go forth, in form, on planet, to restore Love upon sweet Gaia. Each of you came with unique purpose, fully empowered and entirely capable of creating what serves not just your beloved self, but the collective. You are weaving a tapestry where no part of the loom

is untouched—no color excluded, no thread more important than another. The creation is collaborative: above and below, within and without.

"You rebel against coercion, selfishness, greed, and hatred. You embrace freedom—the sovereign right to choose, to be, to create, to share. You are the rebel forces—the rainbow coalition birthing Nova Earth for yourselves and all who follow. You are stepping forward in truth and wisdom, compassion and courage. But stepping forward is the key—in form, on planet, in Love."

This is my invitation, heart to heart, to join me in this Spiritual Rebellion of Love, of Change, of Creation. Take the leap—be a rebel—be a rebel with a cause!

The Invitation to Unity

Unity Did not tiptoe into my consciousness. It arrived with flair—with the passion of a tango, the flair of a flamenco and the grace of a ballet pas de deux. It was present, embodied, and undeniable.

This invitation was not about building castles in the sky but palaces on Earth. Palaces we are invited to inhabit, suffused with the sweet fragrance of roses, jasmine and lilies of the valley, and the fresh air of spring.

Unity didn't demand. It enticed. It beckoned the

senses, whispering joy, play and creation. This is an enchanting invitation impossible to refuse: to unite heart to heart to heart, to join the dance of liberation, to co-create new forms of partnership.

I have never received such a gracious appealing invitation to engage so completely in form, on planet. It was irresistible, appealing to every facet of my sacred self.

And so, from the bottom of my heart I whispered yes.

Saying Yes to Unity

I began this journey with Unity because I was curious and compelled. But I have continued because it is Joy, Wonder, Compassion, Patience, Love—it is everything! It is new, and fresh, filled with Hope and a knowing that this is why I am here. And so, dear reader, I invite you to take this journey with me—to come and join me as we explore and step into Unity Consciousness.

At first, my forays into Unity were with the unseen realms—the Council, the archangels, the Divine Mother. But this seductive invitation was not to travel alone. The call was to join with my fellow humans in an awakening that would elevate all of us into the blossoming, the flowering of who we are in the garden of potential. Although the how was initially unknown, the why felt like the fulfillment of an ancient promise.

Unity is the goal of The Spiritual Rebellion.

And so, beloved reader, I invite you to take this journey with me. To explore. To embody. To step into Unity Heart Consciousness.

Walking in Union

Embracing my role as channel for the Council of Love came after a near-death experience—a turning point that changed everything. It took years not just to accept this calling, but to embody it, to embrace the truth that I am their representative on Earth.

Now I no longer walk alone. I walk in union. The work we have done together on what I call the Unity Project has opened my heart wider than I imagined possible. I am not only a transmitter or scribe; I am in Unity with my beloved unseen friends. I am in sacred partnership with the Council, as they are with me. That is the power of this invitation.

This invitation to step into Unity is for all of us. To acknowledge our human and divine purpose. To experience Love on this planet. To embrace and be the Love, especially with one another, in its radiant array of expressions.

The Awakening

I have always been mission-driven. Whether it was learning the Highland dancing or climbing the corporate ladder, I met each goal with determination. So, imagine the gut-wrenching moment, after that life-altering car accident, when I realized I hadn't yet fulfilled my mission on Earth.

That single moment shifted my world in every conceivable way. I became a foot soldier for the Council. My lifelong connection to Mother Mary deepened to a level of devotion that reshaped my life.

I know beyond a shadow of a doubt, I am loved and valued by the Council. To be chosen for this role is not about ego. It is deeply humbling. To be part of this team even if only as the "water-bearer," an honor.

I share these personal reflections not only to center myself, but to convey the transformative power of what is happening upon Gaia. The Mother has set in motion a reset into Unity. My Great Awakening has been one of awe, reverence and gratitude. Like many, I feel called—summoned—to The Spiritual Rebellion.

But then the question—how could I possibly assist and write about Unity if I haven't experienced it?

Realizing Unity

My aha moment came as I pondered and wrestled with how to approach the vast body of material the COL has given me over the decades. How could I convey the enormity of what is being revealed in a way that individuals and a collective could truly grasp?

It was then the Divine Mother and Archangel Gabrielle came to me, gently nudging, shining light on the realization that Unity Consciousness was already present within me. It had been there for years.

When I channel, I share my sacred space. I stand as a participant-observer, feeling and sensing what the divine being feels, while holding the experience of the person or group. In that moment, separation dissolves.

This doesn't mean I am overtaken or partial to one side or another. I remain vessel of communication. But in that shared field I experience what the Mother pointed out so simply: this is Unity.

Unity is the knowing of another's perspective - feeling their thoughts, emotions, and perceptions in each moment or even across lifetimes. Unity is not manipulation, ownership or control. It is not override. It is intimacy, compassion and connection that shifts perceptions and opens hearts.

Unity allows us to see and offer new perspectives, different pathways. It lets us "walk in another's shoes," if only briefly. It makes us want to help, not to dominate. It is Love in form, in action. A wake-up call to the truth that we are One.

A Deeper Purpose

It is with this deeper sense of purpose that I embark upon this journey with you. Heart to heart to heart. To share what the Council has generously offered about the Mother's reset into Unity.

Each of us carries a unique vision and understanding of Unity, a word that holds a world of meaning. But the Mother is clear: Unity does not mean uniformity. It is not sameness. It is togetherness, harmony, belonging and Love—a sense of intimacy with something greater.

The Mother and the Council of Love now invite us to reach beyond that surface understanding. Unity is not a fleeting state. It is a way of being. A breathing, living expression of connectedness and collective purpose.

Our understanding of Unity has been evolving for years. In The New You (2013) new concepts emerged: Interdimensional Reality, False Grids, Universal Law, the Creation Formula, Sacred Union with Self and Others. Those teachings laid the foundation for how we, as Nova Gaians, live and create within emerging consciousness.

What didn't dawn on me at the time was the fullness of the Mother's divine patterning of sequencing. The breadcrumbs were in front of us all along!

When I finally paused, I was awestruck. With that profound sense of wonder, I chuckled to myself—how did I miss that? Each step, each teaching, each class, had been a careful preparation, guiding us into the next. Always with the Mother's reminder: there is always more.

While I understood the many times we have been told

by our unseen friends in the rafters that the unfoldment was/is in process, the full impact of what was there staring at me on my desk gob-smacked me!

My own personal tendency has always been eyes forward, focusing on the next undertaking. Seldom do I look back to re-examine or review. For me, it's always been onto the next assignment, to what is beckoning just beyond the horizon. That is until now!

Until in this moment of wonder, as I glimpse the magnificence of what has been laid out before us, methodically, gracefully and complete. Each step of our ascension process towards Unity has been divinely titrated, gently guiding us to the next step. How can we possibly forget the Mother's proclamation that there is always more!

If you encounter terms in these chapters that feel new, let them wash over you like a warm tide. You don't need to grasp everything at once. This is not a book of tasks. This is not about adding to your to-do list. It is a book of remembering—layer by layer, heartbeat by heartbeat.

We are not here to escape Earth. We are here to transform it. To transform ourselves. In Unity.

And so, dearheart—let us begin together.

The Progression: A Divine Unfolding

Allow me to share with you some highlights of the

majestic unfolding that began in earnest with the Winter Solstice of December 2022.

For many years now, I've been guided to hold webinars during the solstices and equinoxes—sacred times of energetic shift when the Council of Love offers insight into the deeper unfoldment of the Divine Plan. These gatherings are more than seasonal check-ins; they are markers of the Mother's sequencing, guidance posts in the sacred journey of becoming.

But the Winter Solstice webinar of 2022 Solstice was unlike any before. It was a divine turning point.

Not only did the Divine Mother declare the theme for 2023 to be Harmony, She also revealed that the first quarter of 2023 would initiate a planetary transformation called The Conjunction.

The Conjunction: A Divine Reset

The Conjunction was not symbolic. It was a massive act of divine intercession—the meeting point of time, light, and sound waves of Gaia, colliding with a direct transmission of Source energy from the heart of the Mother.

It was—and is—a planetary reset.

Without fanfare or flashing lights, without most of humanity even realizing it, we were shifted into a new realm of existence. The Mother increased Her quotient of Love-Light on Earth in a way never before seen. The very grid of Gaia was rewoven, and we were invited—gently and irrevocably—into a new vibrational octave.

Some felt it through disrupted sleep or sudden surges of energy. Others felt disoriented, or found unresolved personal and collective issues rising rapidly to the surface. Time itself began to warp—stretching or collapsing—as we moved into this altered reality.

But most clearly, we witnessed the crumbling of what no longer serves. The old grids—death, disease, violence, abuse, ego—can no longer thrive in this frequency. They are surfacing, yes, but only to be cleared. And in their place, something wondrous is rising.

Cracks in the Old Paradigm

Amidst the chaos, there is grace.

There is growing recognition that the old paradigms are done. Grassroots movements are igniting across the globe. People are pushing back against restrictions on their autonomy and choosing sovereignty, equity, and care. Rebellion is not rage—it is a rising.

This is the planetary echo of the inner call: We are ready for something new. We are ready to co-create a world in harmony.

And with that readiness, new gifts began to unfold.

12

Divine Radiance: A Living Grace

The first wave arrived through the Divine Mother Herself—the gift of Divine Radiance.

Although the Council of Love has long spoken of transmitting Divine Radiance and Love, it wasn't until after the Conjunction that I truly felt the magnitude of what this meant. It wasn't just a concept. It was a full-body, soul-deep infusion of Grace.

At first, I wondered, "How did I miss this?" And as always, our beloved Gabrielle answered with loving clarity:

"Because, child, humanity was not yet ready. There were preparatory steps that needed to be taken. The full magnitude of this frequency was too powerful without adequate preparation.

"Unity is a choice—a heart decision made in the full presence of Divine Authority to conjoin with the Love."

Divine Radiance is not simply energy sent from Source. It is the very Grace of God—a radiant, living breath of the Mother's Essence now infusing our fields, our cells, our lives. It awakens the remembrance that our human patterning is born of the divine patterning of the One.

This is not metaphor. It is activation.

And as we are activated, so too are we transformed—not just in who we are, but in how we live and create.

This field of Divine Radiance acts like a sacred sieve. Anything that is not in alignment with Love is transmuted — not with judgment, but with pure light. All is welcome into the field, but not all can remain unchanged. The field itself does the work.

Let yourself feel it now.

Breathe.

Expand.

Open to receive.

Harmonizing: The Dance of Becoming

As this transmission of Divine Radiance deepened, a second theme emerged at the Spring Equinox of 2023: Harmony. Or more precisely, the action of Harmonizing.

Harmonizing is not about sameness. It is not a forced peace or bland consensus. It is the alchemical process of blending energies with Love—infusing all that enters our field with Divine Radiance until balance, beauty, and coherence emerge.

It is an embrace, not a rejection.

Nothing can remain stagnant in the presence of Harmonizing. That which is out of alignment gently transforms—or departs. Either way, the path is cleared.

In our daily lives, this might look like choosing peace over drama. It might be welcoming differences without needing to fix them. It is a conscious choice to live in the energy of Unity—and to create from that frequency.

If this feels abstract, look to nature. The forest does not demand uniformity. It thrives in diversity. Tree, bird, breeze, and sky coexist in elegant communion. Even in movement and change, the song of Harmony resounds.

So breathe it in.

Feel it.

You are not separate from this harmony—you are an essential thread in the weaving.

Sacred Love and Unity: The Next Horizon

It came as no surprise when the Divine Mother then declared the theme for 2024 and 2025 to be Unity. The momentum was clear. The sequencing impeccable.

The Council's newest teachings — particularly around Sacred Love and Unity—have become the centerpiece of this evolving work. The terminology may be new, but the energy is ancient.

When I pause and reflect on the sequencing — the elegant choreography of this progression—I am overcome with awe.

And yes, I smile and ask myself, "How did I miss it?"

But of course, the answer is always the same:
The Mother's Plan has always been perfect.

The Long Arc of Preparation

I now see how each phase of this journey has prepared us for what is now blossoming. The 13th Octave in 1995. The Great Awakening in 2012. The New You in 2013. Each was a gateway, a step deeper into becoming.

The 13th Octave reunited us with the One.

The Great Awakening lit the path.

The New You opened the door to interdimensional living, Universal Law, and Sacred Union.

Now, we are invited to step fully into Unity — not only with Spirit, but with each other. In form. On Earth. As Nova Gaians.

You Are Ready

Has it been an easy road? No.

But it has been sacred.

And it has brought us here.

We are soul-weary from the struggle. We faced our shadows, cleared old grids, and cried out for something more. And now, our hearts—though cautious—are open.

We are not just willing.

We are ready.

Ready to live the Love.

Ready to be the Unity.

Ready to build a world that reflects the truth of who we are.

So, dearheart… As I have invited earlier in this chapter, let us begin. Together.

Chapter Two

What is Unity?

Unity is a Return to Love.

What does Unity have to do with Spiritual Rebellion? Everything.

Unity is the heart of the Spiritual Rebellion—it is the essence, the pulse, the fuel that propels us forward. This rebellion is not merely about what we reject; it is about what we embrace, what we choose to create in ways that do not manipulate, coerce, or control. We are turning away from the systems, beliefs, and patterns that separate us or diminish our sacred creative essence.

And we are turning toward attitudes, actions, and ways of being that uplift, celebrate, and revere the divinity within every person. In Unity, we honor freedom and recognize the sovereignty of all beings.

Unity can be a tricky subject to wrap our arms—and hearts—around. Everyone carries their own understanding of what Unity means, both personally and collectively. But how can we build Nova Earth on Unity if we don't share a common foundation, a shared frequency of comprehension? We must not only understand Unity as a concept, but we must allow ourselves to feel its spirit—its vibration—if we are to emerge into the higher octave of Love and cooperation. Unity is not an idea. It is a living heart, beating vibrantly as we reconstruct Terra Gaia.

It is not enough to know what we are rebelling against. True transformation arises from clarity about what we are moving toward. That clarity is the soil in which lasting change takes root. So let's talk about Unity—not just intellectually, but in the deepest places of our being. Let us explore the path to shared understanding together.

Writing this book—let alone living it—is one of the most challenging things I've ever done. And I wouldn't trade it for the world.

When the Council first spoke of Unity, their words were breathtakingly beautiful. It was like a river of grace washing through my heart and soul with the thrill of possibility. It made me feel hopeful, optimistic, even jubilant. Finally, we—the human collective—were not only poised for a profound paradigm shift but choosing the path of Love.

And then, the world seemed to unravel even further. Chaos ignited on an even greater scale—war, destruction, hatred, violence, abuse. Most disheartening of all was the deepening divisiveness, manifesting in ways I had never witnessed. Fear and pessimism, circular thinking of no way out, defensiveness, polarization exploded. The patterns of manipulation and distortion seemed to be gaining ground and passing as truth and righteousness. And yet, in the midst of this turmoil, the Divine Mother's guidance remained steady: Write. Teach. Focus on Unity. Find the Joy.

It felt extraordinarily challenging, a herculean task in a world where division and conflict is surging to the surface like a volcanic eruption. I couldn't help but wonder if I am voice crying in the wilderness, deluded by my own heart's desires, the court jester or the pathfinder. Was I delusional or way ahead of my time? These questions were a decision point for me, a juncture that we are all indeed facing.

But here was the biggest challenge: to write about Unity, I could not merely understand it. I had to become it. I had to integrate its essence into every thought, word and choice. And that, dearheart, has been one of the greatest challenges of my lifetime.

There were times I was weary and disheartened. Times I set the work aside to rest, to heal, to whisper to the Mother, Is this really the way? And always the answer returned:

"Yes, beloved. Keep going. You are not alone."

So I did.

Unity is not for a chosen few. It is for everyone. It cannot be otherwise.

The Challenge of Becoming

It is no accident that Unity arises just as chaos breaks wide open.

We cannot build a world that works for everyone until we see—clearly and unflinchingly—what does not. The wars, the violence, the bitter divides are not signs of failure. They are wounds rising to the surface to be healed.

This unearthing of our collective wounds—is part of our collective shift to a higher frequency of being. This is the challenge to each and every one of us.

If patterns of ego and self-interest remain buried, they thrive. If discourse dissolves into camps, common ground erodes. If we cease to truly hear one another, alienation deepens.

Unity asks us to see, not to judge. To choose, again and again, Love over fear. Connection over isolation.

Understanding this is one thing. Living it is another. To step back, to be the observer rather than the reactor, to hold the vision of love while maintaining Divine Neutrality—this is no small feat.

Unity is an invitation extended to all—inclusive, engaging, creative, and yes, at times, one of the greatest challenges we will ever face.

And so, with that heartfelt declaration, welcome to this journey into the heart of Unity!

The Universal Drive

Much has been written about human needs—Maslow's hierarchy of survival and self-actualization. Yet beneath it all lies something simpler and more profound:

We are wired to give, receive, and be Love.

In current societies, emphasis is often placed on differences and the value of individuality. Yet, beneath this surface, there are profound commonalities that define us all.

This yearning precedes survival. It is encoded in our very DNA. When ego takes the stage, when cruelty flares, it is often not malice at the root, but a distortion of longing. A cry for Love unmet.

When we witness behaviors that seem aberrant, whether personal or global, they often stem from a yearning for love or a reaction to its perceived absence. When ego takes center stage, it reflects an experience of love unrecognized or unmet. The drive to love and be loved precedes even our most basic survival instincts. It is as intrinsic as breathing.

A lack of self-worth, for instance, arises from a denial of self-love or a history devoid of loving experiences.

Yet, this universal truth remains: there is not one among us who does not yearn for Love. Denying this truth is often a shield against pain, but the deeper impulse—to reconnect with Love's divine essence within ourselves and the greater whole—is unshakable. It compels us to gather, to form community, and to seek Unity.

No one is exempt from this truth. Every one of us, no matter how shielded, yearns to love and be loved.

Acknowledging this stand-alone truth, we explore what Unity and Unity Consciousness truly mean, why they matter, and how they form the foundation of Earth's new operating system. Together, we'll delve into the essence of Unity, uncovering its meaning, its pathway, and the power it holds for all of us.

Unity is not a distant ideal but as a lived experience waiting to unfold. Are you ready to step into this adventure?

The Experience of Unity

To live in Unity Consciousness is to recognize this shared yearning. To know what aches in me also aches in you.

Unity is knowing of another's perspective—feeling their thoughts, emotions, and perceptions, whether in a moment or across lifetimes. It is not ownership or control. It is compassion. Intimacy. A willingness to walk briefly in another's shoes.

Unity is woven of many sacred threads: harmony, sacred love, divine neutrality, vulnerability, courage, balance. None stand alone. They harmonize—as we are meant to.

Unity is, in its essence, a collective experience. To embody Unity means recognizing these sacred qualities within us, allowing them to flow and work in harmony. In Unity, these aspects join in a beautiful purpose, reflecting our highest example of interconnection.

Unity changes everything. It is Love in form, in action. A genuine wake-up call to the truth that we are, indeed, One.

The Mother tells us:

> "Unity is the surrender, acceptance, and embrace that you are part and parcel, an integral part of the heart, mind, being, and existence of One, God, Source, All. It is far more than a sense of being. It is being in the full connectedness and balance of every particle of your beautiful sacred self with All."

This is not abstraction. This is reality.

Embracing Unity Consciousness means recognizing this shared drive for Love and connectedness. It invites us to expand our understanding of what it means to be human and to co-create as Nova Gaians in this transformative age. The question then becomes: How do we embody Unity in our daily lives, and what do we mean when we speak of it?

For Unity to flourish, there must be a collective understanding—rooted not only in esoteric ideals but also in practical applications. This shared understanding is the foundation of co-creating a world that works for everyone.

Unity as the Third Rail

The Council calls Unity the "third rail"—not something to fear, but the vital current that powers Love into form. It is the heartbeat of Nova Earth.

Regardless of race, gender, or nationality, we all seek solutions to the crises that plague our world: war, violence, abuse, disrespect, despair, and loneliness. These challenges are symptoms of disconnection—from love, from each other, and from our divine essence. Unity is the solution.

Unity is not only mystical; it is practical.

It looks like kindness.
It sounds like deep listening.
It feels like inclusion, even when we disagree.

> "Unity is heart consciousness… the deep recognition that all things, all energy, is united and that separation is but an old illusion." — Council of Love

Beyond Time

Unity is not confined to time or space. It is interdimensional. It flows across timelines, across realms, across dimensions. And so do you.

> "Unity is being the Infinity of One—the Never Ending Wonderful of All — the ability to flow in and out of and through time." — Council of Love

Unity invites us to drop the illusion of separation, to soften, to stop insisting on being right.

> "It's not about acquiescing to someone else's priorities but making the divinely neutral decision that being united is more important than being right — that love is more important than any ego position or desire. Our opinions don't grow corn." — Council of Love

This is not passivity. It is presence. It is choosing to live from a new operating system where Love is not just a sentiment, but the foundation of reality.

Living in Unity means immersing ourselves in the beauty and wonders of Love, harmonizing with Gaia's offerings and each other. It's a full-hearted, joyful participation:

> "It is the full participation, equally and joyfully, in all the wonders of Love that Gaia offers, and that you are capable and willing to experience. It is the knowing that

each dimension, and that each of the 12 planes within each dimension, offers a splendor of heart expansion and embrace. It is a knowing that every person, every being, brings that unique experience of Love, of the unique experience of One."

Unity is the recognition that all things, all beings, all energy are intrinsically connected. It's a deep heart consciousness that sees separation as an illusion of the past. This does not mean abandoning our individuality but choosing Love over ego, connection over the need to be right.

The Mother's Question

The Divine Mother never leaves us with only teachings. She leaves us with a question to ponder, to feel, to delve into.

These are not simply questions but invitations—doors to inner exploration, encouraging us to draw from the well of our mind, heart, and soul, bringing that light into our everyday interactions.

Each question is designed as a catalyst for clearing anything that might cloud our connection to Unity, using both your willingness and Divine Mother's Radiance to dissolve any lingering layers or unresolved energies.

"Beloved, how are you in Unity with your sacred self? Where is the You in Unity?"

27

When the Mother first asked me this question, I was unraveled. I had never truly paused to ask. And when I did, which took time, it rearranged me.

This is not a question for the mind, but for the soul.

Sit with it. Let it whisper in your heart. Allow it to reveal not words, but a feeling. A remembrance.

You do not need to fix anything. Just be willing. Allow the Radiance of the Mother to do the rest.

We are in this together. And Unity, beloved, is already within you.

Chapter Three

Humanity's Journey to Unity

Change rarely arrives like lightning. It unfolds like dawn—first a glow on the horizon, then light spilling slowly across sky and earth. Humanity's shift to Unity is just such a dawn. It is the It begins in our hearts, ripples through communities, and only then reshapes our structures and systems.

Archangel Michael once said:

"We are seeding the planet with those willing and strong enough to anchor the New — to join in community and create this Planet of Love where war and abuse are not even options."

The Soil of Change

Cultural change is the soil. It is where new values take root.

Civic change is the sprout—those values made visible through shared action.

Political change is the flowering—structures and policies that reflect what culture has already embraced.

And beneath it all lies the foundation: Universal Law. The Laws of Love. The truths that remind us of our interconnectedness.

Sanat Kumara counsels:

> "You are laying down the new paradigm — kindness, gentleness, consideration — through the application of Universal Law. It is not about ascendancy but about creating a world where the sovereignty of every being is honored."

This is how the Mother's Plan unfolds: in sequence. Cultural change, then civic change, then political change. Each stage is necessary. Each step divinely designed.

In this chapter, we'll explore how meaningful, lasting transformation arises on personal, cultural, and global levels. This isn't just a random process; it's divinely guided, flowing from the grassroots—beginning with individuals like you and me—through our communities, and outward into cultural, civic, and political realms.

By divine design, this shift into Unity Consciousness honors free will. It invites each of us to actively participate in co-creating a world built on shared values of justice, compassion, and equality. Together, we'll reflect on the essential markers along humanity's journey and how each step brings us closer to realizing Unity as envisioned by the Divine.

From Cultural Change to Civic Engagement to Political Evolution

Have you ever found yourself wrestling with a deep question, searching for clarity on how profound peace or genuine Unity might take root in our world? I certainly have. For years, I've pondered how humanity could move from division to wholeness, wondering what sequence of changes—within hearts, minds, and societies—would need to unfold for Unity to truly become the foundation of Nova Earth.

My own aha moment came during the 2024 U.S. presidential election season. While watching a broadcast featuring David Brooks, a journalist with the New York Times, he illuminated something simple yet profound: lasting collective change begins with cultural transformation. From there, it grows into civic engagement and ultimately blossoms into political evolution.

That insight reminded me to return my focus to the starting point: cultural change. As someone deeply immersed in later stages of this evolution, I had overlooked this vital first step. And yet, it's here—in the quiet, grassroots movements of hearts and communities—that the values of Unity take root.

Our task, as co-creators of Nova Earth, is clear: we

must nurture these seeds of cultural change. Only then can they grow into civic engagement and, eventually, political systems and governance rooted in justice, compassion, and equity.

When I pause and remind myself of our shared role as pathfinders and wayshowers, the sequencing makes perfect sense. As angels and agents of change, we are forging a new path ahead. And we are not alone; I take heart in the countless shifts already happening. Across the globe, civic movements for fairness and equity are thriving. Genuine leaders and individuals alike are laboring for justice and compassion at every level of community and nationhood.

Humanity's evolution is not just a biological unfolding; it's a spiritual and social transformation shaped by culture, action, and governance. It begins with the values we share, grows through collective action, and culminates in systems that reflect the harmony of Unity Consciousness. Together, let's delve into how these shifts are already happening—and how we can continue to walk this path as co-creators of a better world.

Cultural Change: The Seed of Transformation

Cultural change is where our evolution begins. At its core, culture is a collection of shared attitudes, values, goals, and practices that define who we are and what we value. Our beliefs shape the stories we tell, the behaviors we consider acceptable, and the way we interpret our place in the world. When cultural change occurs, it signals a shift in our collective consciousness, a rethinking of the norms that guide us. This is where transformation takes root.

Cultural evolution often starts subtly, with shifts in ideas and attitudes, and gradually gains momentum. These changes can come from individuals, artists, or thinkers who challenge norms through art, writing, or activism. Their ideas often inspire others to question long-held beliefs and to reconsider what is possible. From Renaissance humanism to the digital revolution, cultural evolution has been the precursor to social transformation.

One powerful example of cultural change is the gradual but powerful shift towards embracing diversity and inclusiveness. This shift has transformed not only how we interact with each other but also how we see ourselves as a global family. The ripple effect of cultural changes—such as movements for equality, mental health awareness, environmental responsibility, and social justice—creates the conditions for civic engagement and political shifts to come.

Civic Engagement: Transforming Culture into Action

Civic engagement is where cultural beliefs turn into action. While culture is the fertile soil, it is in civic engagement that we actively embody and advocate for the changes we want to see. This is the stage where values transform into behaviors, and where individuals come together to create communities that reflect their evolving beliefs.

Civic engagement encompasses a wide range of activities, from grassroots organizing, volunteering, and community building to advocacy and social movements. When individuals act together based on shared values, they amplify their voice, bringing cultural ideals to life.

This stage of engagement builds networks of shared purpose—we begin to build the garden. From labor unions to climate action groups, grassroots organizations are born here. They provide a structure for hope and determination to sprout—for individuals to unite under common causes and advocate for policy changes that mirror shifting cultural values. Consider, for instance, the civil rights movements around the world. These movements began with a shift in cultural beliefs regarding equality and justice and transformed into powerful networks of civic action. Through rallies, boycotts, and protests, people demanded an end to discriminatory practices and laws. These efforts made it clear to policymakers that society had changed, requiring real and lasting transformation.

As we step into this sacred work of transformation, Mother Mary's call to action resonates deeply:

"This is my call to action. Each and every day, in all realms, all behaviors, all industries, in everything you do, you do it in my name as I do it in yours. You are born creator from Creator Source. Let us proceed as family. Let us assist, not only the humans, the animals, the elements, let us assist our beloved Gaia in being allowed to demonstrate and fulfill the totality of who she is."

Her words remind us that civic engagement is not just about addressing human concerns but about embracing the fullness of our shared responsibility as co-inhabitants of Earth. It is about honoring all life—human, animal, elemental—and supporting Gaia herself in fulfilling her divine purpose.

When we approach civic action with this profound understanding, we step forward as co-creators of a world rooted in love, justice, and harmony. Together, we embody the sacred values of Nova Earth, helping humanity and Gaia flourish as one unified family.

Political Change: Embodying New Values in Law

Political change is the culmination of cultural and civic evolution. It is the stage where collective beliefs and grassroots action translate into policies, laws, and institutional reforms. Political structures are often slower to change than culture or civic actions because they represent the codified, structural foundation of society.

However, political change is essential to anchoring the values of an evolving culture in law.

Political evolution occurs when new policies are enacted that reflect the shifts in public values and collective consciousness. When civic movements gain enough momentum, they have the power to influence political leaders, inspiring changes that impact the legal, economic, and social fabric of society. Laws that once seemed unchangeable—such as those governing segregation, gender discrimination, or marriage equality—are transformed as society evolves.

Political change, however, is not the endpoint; rather, it acts as a reinforcing mechanism that sustains cultural shifts over time. When laws and policies are updated to reflect new cultural values, they further support the cultural and civic structures that advocated for these changes. They become the foundation upon which future generations build, creating a more inclusive, compassionate, and just society.

The Interplay Between Cultural, Civic, and Political Change

The evolution from cultural to civic to political change is not linear but linked—interconnected. Cultural beliefs shape civic actions, civic engagement pushes for political change, and political change, in turn, reinforces cultural values. This cycle is ongoing, as each stage influences and propels the others forward. New cultural shifts continue to arise, prompting fresh civic engagement and, eventually, further political evolution. This dynamic interplay is what drives human progress, helping society adapt to new challenges and expand its capacity for compassion and justice.

In this interconnected cycle, we also see the importance of each stage. Cultural change alone, without civic or political engagement, remains in the realm of ideas and ideals. Civic engagement, without cultural backing, can lack the momentum and collective support needed to sustain change. And political change, if not grounded in genuine cultural and civic transformation, can lack authenticity and fail to resonate with the broader population.

The Role of Individuals in the Cycle of Change

At each stage of this evolutionary process, individual contributions matter deeply. Each of us plays a role in shaping cultural beliefs, participating in civic actions, and influencing political change. By embracing new values and participating in collective action, individuals contribute to the broader cultural and civic shifts that lead to political transformation. Whether through conversations, art, community involvement, or political advocacy, even civil disobedience, every action contributes to the larger tapestry of human evolution.

When we think of cultural change, civic engagement, and political evolution as an interconnected process, we recognize our own power in shaping society. The small, everyday decisions we make, how we treat others, the conversations we engage in, the causes we support—are all part of this evolutionary cycle. Each of us, as active participants in this journey, holds the potential to make an impact that goes far beyond ourselves, influencing the values and structures that guide future generations.

Harmonizing with Evolution

As we continue to evolve culturally, civically, and politically, we are invited to harmonize with this natural progression. This harmonization asks us to engage with our communities, advocate for our beliefs, and support political changes that reflect our deepest values. By aligning with this evolutionary process, we create a society that resonates with compassion, unity, and justice—a society that reflects the love and values we hold within.

In recognizing the powerful interplay between culture, civic engagement, and politics, we see that human evolution is not simply about adapting to change but about consciously creating it. Each step forward is a testament to our shared humanity and the ever-deepening capacity of our collective spirit to envision and create a better world.

From Cultural Change to Civic Action to Political Evolution—The Influence of Universal Law

In our exploration of how humanity evolves from cultural change to civic engagement to political transformation, we must consider the profound influence of Universal Law.

Sanat Kumara explains:

"Universal Law is not merely a codification to sit in a library. It is not the purview of old men and rigid beings in gowns to dictate to anybody. Universal Law—the Universal Laws of Love—is a code of behavior. They are the standard upon which everything is measured, and everything is built. It is the expression of behavior of heart, of heart listening, heart speaking, heart engagement. It is how communities, communities of all, and communities of One come together to operate… to work, to play, to pray, to build, to restore."

This set of principles, often referred to as the Laws of Love, serves as both a guide and a foundation for the shifts we experience at each stage of evolution. Universal Law acts as the underlying framework that shapes our understanding of our interconnectedness and responsibilities toward one another and the world.

The Foundation of Universal Law

Universal Law is rooted in the understanding that all beings are interconnected. It teaches us that our actions resonate beyond ourselves and that every thought, word, and deed have a ripple effect on the collective consciousness. At its core, Universal Law embodies principles such as love, harmony, balance, and respect for all living beings. This foundational knowledge is crucial for navigating the journey from cultural to civic to political change, as it informs our choices and interactions with the world around us.

As we consider the dynamics of cultural change, it is important to recognize that shifts in collective beliefs often stem from a growing awareness of these Universal Laws. Cultural evolution invites individuals to reflect on their values and understand their impact on the larger community. For example, movements advocating for social justice, environmental sustainability, and equality often emerge from a collective realization of our interconnectedness and shared responsibility, as guided by Universal Law.

Cultural Change: Awakening to Universal Truths

Cultural change begins when individuals awaken to the deeper truths that Universal Law reveals. This awakening leads to a shift in collective consciousness, inspiring new ways of thinking and being. As individuals align their beliefs with the principles of Universal Law, cultural narratives begin to change, creating an environment ripe for civic engagement.

When we recognize that love, compassion, and harmony are not just ideals but essential elements of our existence, we begin to reshape our cultural landscape. This re imagining can manifest in various forms, such as art, literature, and social movements, all aimed at fostering greater understanding and connection among people. The Council of Love emphasizes that as we engage in alignment with Universal Law, we not only transform our internal world but also catalyze broader societal shifts.

Civic Engagement: Living the Laws of Love

As cultural change takes root, civic engagement emerges as a natural response. When individuals feel inspired by the principles of Universal Law, of fundamentally what feels right or wrong; fair or unfair; of love or not, they seek to embody these values in their communities. Civic engagement becomes a way to put love and compassion into action, demonstrating the interconnectedness of all beings and the importance of collective responsibility.

In this context, civic action becomes a powerful expression of Universal Law. Grassroots movements, community initiatives, and social justice efforts reflect the desire to align societal structures with the deeper truths of love, equality, and harmony. The Council of Love reminds us that civic engagement is not merely about seeking change but about embodying the very essence of the Law of Love in our relationships with others and the world.

When we engage civically, we invite others to join us in creating a harmonious community that reflects the principles of Universal Law. This process fosters collaboration and understanding, allowing diverse voices and perspectives to coexist and contribute to the greater good. It reminds us that every act of kindness, every effort to uplift others, is a manifestation of those Laws in action.

Political Change: Transforming Structures with Universal Principles

Political evolution is the culmination of cultural and civic engagement and deeply influenced by Universal Law. When communities mobilize around shared values and principles, they gain the momentum necessary to inspire political change. Laws and policies that emerge from this process are often reflections of the collective consciousness that has been shaped by cultural and civic engagement.

Universal Law plays a critical role in this stage of evolution by guiding our understanding of justice, equality, and the common good. The COL teaches us that true political change goes beyond mere policy reform; it requires a transformation of the underlying beliefs that govern our institutions. As we advocate for policies that align with Universal Law, rather than laws based on self-interest, we create a political landscape that reflects the love, harmony, and respect we seek in our society.

This alignment between political action and Universal Law allows us to address systemic issues that have long persisted. It challenges us to question established norms and to seek reforms that uplift the marginalized and promote the well-being of all. By grounding our political aspirations in Universal Law, we create a more just and equitable society, one that honors the intrinsic worth of every individual.

The Interconnected Dance of Change

The interplay between cultural change, civic engagement, and political evolution is enriched by our understanding of Universal Law. Each stage of this evolutionary process is interconnected, with Universal Law serving as the guiding force that shapes our actions and intentions. As we recognize our shared humanity and embrace the principles of love and harmony, we create a cycle of change that reflects the best of who we are.

We are not merely passive observers in this process

but active participants who hold the power to shape our reality. By embodying the principles of Universal Law in our daily lives, we contribute to the cultural shifts that inspire civic engagement and drive political transformation. This interconnected dance of change invites us to step into our roles as agents of love and harmony, guiding the evolution of our society.

Sanat Kumara guides us in this pivotal moment of transformation:

"You are in a very dramatic time of transition. You, as the collective, are being asked to step forward and declare the injustice, the lack of love, which permeates so many of your systems. What you are doing is laying down the new paradigm, and you are showing and demonstrating literally/physically/materially what is possible. Each of you, in various ways, are being asked to step forth and in fact declare where fairness, where the balance, where the ability to stay in a unified grid of love and heart... where that rests. It is not about ascendancy, or preferential treatment of one being over another.

"It quite literally is creating a world where kindness and gentleness, consideration and laughter, sweetness and sharing are the watchwords, are the operational principles where the sovereignty of the individual is honored, not dismissed. How you are doing this is, of course, from the sweetness of your being, from the gentleness of your being, from the love of your heart, the brilliance of your mind, and through the application of Universal Law."

Sanat Kumara's words remind us that we are not simply witnessing the changes happening in the world—we are co-creators in them. We are called to stand for justice, fairness, and love, to ensure that the new paradigm we are laying down is one that honors the sovereignty of every being and reflects the fullness of our divine potential. By embodying Universal Law in our actions, we lay the foundation for a society rooted in kindness, respect, and unity.

As we continue to engage in this interconnected dance of cultural, civic, and political transformation, let us remember that each of us plays a vital role in manifesting the world we envision—a world where love, fairness, and harmony are the operational principles that guide all of us.

Harmonizing with Universal Law

As we navigate the journey from cultural change to civic action to political evolution, we are invited to harmonize with Universal Law. This harmonization requires us to reflect on our beliefs, engage with our communities, and advocate for policies that align with the deeper truths of love and interconnectedness. In doing so, we create a society that embodies the essence of Universal Law and Unity Consciousness—a society that honors the dignity of all beings and fosters a sense of unity and purpose.

In recognizing the profound influence of Universal Law, we see that our journey of evolution is not merely a personal endeavor but a collective mission. By embracing these principles, we contribute to a larger movement toward understanding, compassion, and justice, creating a world that reflects the love we hold within. This is the essence of our evolution as humans: to rise together, guided by the light of Love—of Universal Law, into a future that honors our interconnectedness and shared responsibility.

Yes, It's Personal

When we glimpse the scale of this shift, it can feel completely overwhelming. How do we get from fractured systems to a world where Love is the norm? As we look around and see, feel, observe the chaos we can't help but wonder, what difference does one person make?

The Council's answer is always simple: one act, one choice, one heart at a time.

Your role is not to move mountains in a day. Your role is to live Love in the small, ordinary moments. To choose kindness. To choose fairness. To choose compassion.

Every gesture plants a seed in the collective field.

Unity is not a grand gesture or heroic feat. It is daily becoming. It is remembering—together.

Yes, the structures of the world are changing. Yes, the old systems are dissolving. But beneath it all, what is happening is deeply human: a memory of our shared essence.

And the Council's promise is steady, simple, and sure:

You are not alone. And Love is winning

The Mother's Question

The Divine Mother asks:

"Where in your daily life can you choose being united over being right? Where can you soften, beloved, into Love?"

These are not abstract questions. They are invitations to practice.

In the moment you feel the urge to defend, can you pause? In the moment you want to retreat, can you soften instead? In the moment you feel like retreating can you stay still and hold the Love? Because dearheart, these are the thresholds where Unity is born.

Chapter Four

Where Are We? What's Really Going On

I am never alone—and neither are you. To be surrounded by the Council of Love is both miraculous and humbling. Their presence reminds me that even in the turbulence of these times, Heaven and Earth are intertwined, and we are profoundly guided.

And yet, my purpose as the COL's representative on Earth requires me to remain anchored, steady, present on terra firma. It is not always easy. The work of Unity cannot unfold in the heavens alone; it must root here, in our daily lives, our cultures, our civic engagement, and even in politics. That means we must face, honestly and tenderly, the landscape of where we are right now.

Profound awareness of the global environment, the temperament, the challenges, and the collective mood of the planet—is essential in discerning how to move forward. From one perspective, it seems obvious: wars, climate crisis, political instability, autocracy, inequality, loneliness. The heartbreak of our world is undeniable.

Seeing with New Eyes

But there is also a subtler current—the Mother's Divine Sequencing. This is not random chaos. It is a pattern, a rhythm beneath the surface, guiding us toward alignment with Love. Sometimes it moves like a gentle tide, almost imperceptible. Other times it rushes in like a rip current, demanding our attention. Both currents are equally impactful in understanding and working with the unfoldment of the Divine Universal Plan

Both currents are essential, part of the unfoldment of the Plan. Understanding this flow allows us to step into our role as conscious co-creators, working in harmony with these divine energies as we journey toward Unity Heart Consciousness.

When we notice these patterns, we shift from being passive witnesses of upheaval to conscious co-creators with the Divine.

The Mother says:

"Beloved children, in this era of awakening, you are beginning to see beyond the individual self. The signs of change surround you, woven into the air you breathe, the relationships you cherish, and the world you build."

The Signs of Change

Extreme weather. Social upheaval. Shifts in consciousness. These are not only crises, but signals. Gaia is speaking. The collective is speaking.

The Mother and the Council remind us: real change comes from the grassroots. From each of us. From the daily decisions we make, rooted in our free will and our divine authority.

There is no denying the current serious social, environmental, and political issues we face: climate change, autocracy, political instability and divisiveness, food and water insecurity, technological disruption, poverty, and inequality. These vast challenges require a comprehensive shift in how we, as inhabitants of Earth, behave, where we place our priorities, and what actions we choose to take.

The COL has long shared that the changes upon Gaia will—and must—come from the grassroots. This paradigm shift builds from the bottom up, through our collective free will choices and the divine authority we exercise in creating Nova Gaia. This paradigm shift is based upon the prowess of our heart consciousness, decisions and subsequent creative decisions and actions that consider not only our intellectual power but our core wisdom as divine sovereign beings.

And yet, the Mother does not leave us mired in imbalance. Her gaze is always forward. She points to what we are building, what is already being born.

This is why we examine issues like the epidemic of loneliness, a poignant signal of what needs to shift urgently. The widespread feelings of isolation, exclusion, exhaustion, disillusionment, and powerlessness reflect our need to move from surviving to thriving. Loneliness is not only an individual ache—it is a collective signpost. It reveals how urgently we must move from survival into connection, from separation into Unity.

Our collective and individual hearts are demanding these shifts to systems and patterns that are considerate and cognizant of the demands of our hearts.

The Divine focus, however, is not merely on what is out of balance, but on where we are headed, what we are co-creating. The light of a new day, a new consciousness, is already upon us. Now, it's our gift and our responsibility to choose how we will heal, thrive, claim and build the lives we desire and deserve. This is what the Council of Love calls part of our divine inheritance.

Personal Reflection: Recognizing Divine Patterns

I will not pretend I am untouched by what I see. There are moments when the weight of war, violence, hunger, and arrogance overwhelms me. I have wept for children displaced, for the cruelty of bigotry, for the imbalance of power. At times, the lone voice crying in the wilderness.

But in those moments, I do what I know: I go into my heart. I send Love, energy, healing. I tend to my own sacred vulnerability. And I call upon the Company of Heaven: Please, send help.

This, too, is part of the journey—to feel deeply, to not deny sorrow, and to let Love flow through it all.

But as we navigate these changing seas, it's important not to stay in overwhelm but to also recognize the sacred signs of transformation. In the shifting climate, in social movements, and in our personal challenges, every experience is an opportunity to align with the Divine patterns unfolding around us.

Take a few moments to pause and reflect on the divine patterns you are noticing. What has been catching your attention, calling you? What global patterns are standing out to you? What personal patterns are you yearning to shift? How are you choosing to move into greater alignment with your unique divine patterning, and with the divine sequencing already underway?

The Essence of Divine Sequencing

Divine Sequencing is the heartbeat of Creation. It is how the Universe unfolds, step by step, often beyond our awareness of time. Even when something feels absent, it may already be present on higher planes, waiting for our consciousness to catch up.

The Mother's recent "reset" brings a new level of

fluidity, where dimensional boundaries are merging into our conscious awareness, allowing us to participate more fully in this unfolding.

From the dawn of Gaia's birth, Sequencing has been at work. From the 13th Octave to humanity's choice to ascend together in 2012, to the Mother's Pause in 2020, to the Conjunction of 2022–23; each has been a step in the pattern. Each has carried us into the Mother's New Normal.

And now, the theme She has given us for since 2024 through 2026 is Unity. A theme that will not fade but deepen, guiding us into heart consciousness as the foundation of Nova Earth.

Her words for this time are clear:

> "Unity continues. It is a theme of Unity, Hope, and Action! … The Nova is Heart Consciousness. It is a living, and it is a valuing of the importance of Love in all its wonderful array of expressions. Unity comes from the grassroots. It comes from each and every one of you."

Humanity's Awakening

As we heed this call to Unity, we may find ourselves experiencing a significant inner shift. Unity Consciousness asks us to relinquish anything misaligned with Love, to allow any lingering discord to dissolve, and to welcome a sense of wholeness.

Archangel Michael has shared:

"The layers and layers of illusion and delusion that have been laid upon this planet by the human collective have created such an illusion of reality, of restriction and compulsion, and none of it is real. All it does and all it has done is hold the each of you, and the collective, in a web of deceit. That web has been broken. It is not that it is about to be broken. It is not that you are even in the midst of it being broken. It is broken. It is dissolving!"

In unity, we stand together, guided by Gaia's rhythms and the Divine. Each step brings us deeper into a shared vision of Sacred Love—one that transcends the illusions of separation and highlights our intrinsic connection to every being.

Archangel Michael offers insight into this shift, describing it as a public awakening toward Love. He speaks of this third rail path beyond right and wrong, beyond duality, where love becomes our unifying principle. As we awaken, our hearts yearn for an existence rooted in unity, a world where each action is inspired by love.

Our collective journey with Divine Sequencing spans millennia, a dance toward the dawn of a new world, Nova Gaia. Throughout history, specific moments have acted as catalysts for awakening, marking stillpoints of reflection, such as the solstices and equinoxes. These moments are embedded in Gaia's rhythms and flow through us as sacred opportunities for balance, rebirth, and alignment with the cosmic pulse of life.

The theme of Unity will only strengthen and grow over the coming years. This is the part of not only divine sequencing but the divine invitation to personal growth and transformation, to a life that is richer, rewarding, productive and inclusive.

We cannot create Unity in isolation, that would be a contradiction in the very essence of this energy. And we do not travel alone, regardless of how far we may think we have veered off course, the Mother guides us:

"There are lessons learned when one travels collectively or individually into the darkness. But the only reason you go into the darkness is to discover the light, to discover the magnificence, the radiance of all the rays, of All, and of all of you!

"Unity is the assumption of your Divine Authority, but more than that, of your deepest, passionate heart's desire—the heart desire to know, to be, to experience, to express freely, unreservedly, Love.

"Unity is the change to heartset! Heart Consciousness is the awareness, living, and valuing of the importance of Love in all its wonderful array of expressions.

"Unity envelops neutrality, not by abolishing discernment, but by realizing, embracing that the genuine wisdom of direction already rests within you. The only litmus test is within you... AND... Is it of Love?"

Gaia's Voice: A Call to Co-Create

Gaia, our beloved Earth Mother, also speaks. Through storms, tides, winds, and seasons, she calls us back into balance. These signals are not punishments. They are reminders of the sacred contract between humanity and Earth.

In partnership with Gaia, we co-create Nova Earth, recognizing her as Gi'Anna, the Jewel in the Mother's Crown.

The Divine Mother's vision for Earth is as a haven where all beings can experience physical form in unity, harmony, and love. She reminds us that our purpose is to live fully as our Divine selves, aware of our connection to every living thing. Our lives, aligned with the sacred rhythms of Gaia, are a testament to this unity.

Gaia herself, our beloved Earth Mother, speaks to us through her cycles and rhythms. Through her own transformation, she guides humanity to reconnect with the natural world.

"Through the movement of the tides, the whispers of

the wind, and the rhythm of the seasons, Gaia calls you to remember your ancient bond with her. Each sign is a call to return to balance."

To respond to Gaia's signals, we can integrate practices that honor our relationship with the Earth. This might mean reducing waste, spending time in nature, or adopting habits that support sustainability. As we align with her rhythms, we support the healing of the planet and our collective journey toward unity.

As Gaia thrives, so do we. Our interconnectedness is undeniable, our well-being in every facet of our lives depends upon the care and nurturing of this sacred relationship. It is not merely a matter of maintenance—it is a matter of repair and honoring of the fractured relationship, which in so many ways is indicative of humanity's disconnect from self.

Personal Reflection: Morning Light

One of my greatest joys has always been walking my dog early in the morning. To step out into the hush of a new day and feel the cool air kiss my skin… to hear the gentle rustle of leaves and the sweet songs of the birds greeting the dawn… to watch the water birds quietly stalk the shallows while my pup revels in the simple wonder of just being alive—this touches something ancient and sacred within me. It anchors a deep inner knowing: peace is not only possible, it's already present.

For years, I wondered how I could share this precious, everyday grace with others — not to teach, not to narrate, but simply to share the moment, the stillness, the beauty that so freely opens my heart and reminds me of why I'm grateful to be here on this planet.

And so, I began taking simple "morning light" photos on my walks. A single rose in bloom. The golden shimmer on a leaf. A cloud lit with lavender. A bunny hiding in shadow. A heron poised in silence. These aren't dramatic vistas or curated scenes—just snippets of wonder from my suburban morning. A whisper from Gaia. A glimpse of the sacred.

For over a decade, I've quietly shared these snapshots on social media. No captions. No commentary. Just heart-sharing. And in doing so, I've realized this daily ritual is more than a habit—it's a living prayer. A small but powerful act of honoring Gaia. Of gratitude. Of connection.

The most miraculous part? It never stops bringing me joy.

Each time, I receive the gift of Gaia's beauty anew.

Then I receive the gift of sharing it.

Then the gift of connection — with old friends and new, with those who pause to say, "Yes… I see it too."

And just like that, we are united—not by politics or belief systems or cultural norms—but by our shared reverence for this magnificent planet we call home.

This is how Gaia heals us, teaches us, and draws us back into balance — one tender moment at a time.

What simple, joy-filled practice can you begin—and truly stick with—that deepens your relationship with Gaia?

What physical or esoteric ritual might speak to your heart… something that brings a smile to your belly, a quiet thrill of connection, a sense of peace woven into your daily rhythm?

What calls to you?

Start there.

It will feed your soul. I promise.

A Vision of Unity

Archangel Jophiel, Keeper of Time, calls our journey into Unity a grand adventure. He invites us to step into the infinite connection of Love, to know ourselves as brilliant threads in the tapestry of the One.

This is not abstract. It is practical. Unity asks us to surrender what is not of Love. To choose compassion over judgment. To walk the "third rail"—beyond duality, into Love as our unifying principle.

"I invite you to journey into the infinite connection of

love, to experience the Divine Essence of One, and to know yourself fully in the brilliance of your soul. You are not separate from each other, nor from the Earth. Each thought, word, and deed reverberates, weaving you together in an endless flow of connection and purpose."

In this invitation, Jophiel asks us to step beyond the illusion of separation and realize that unity is our true nature, our destined path of infinite potential.

In Unity Consciousness, we recognize that our actions, thoughts, and intentions affect the whole. Archangel Jophiel's message encourages us to nurture a mindset of togetherness and to see the divine purpose in our shared journey.

In response to this call to Unity, many of us are experiencing intense shifts. Unity Consciousness asks us to surrender everything not aligned with Love and Unity, allowing discord to surface for release. It's an invitation to shift from paradigms of separation to a new understanding of wholeness.

This is not a solitary path; we walk it together, with the Divine and each other. Building on the theme of Harmony, we join Gaia's invitation to rebalance, harmonize, and attune to a smoother, gentler rhythm infused with the Mother's essence. This journey has brought us to the next step: Unity Consciousness and Sacred Love.

Core Elements of Unity

Unity is structured around key elements that hold us to this path and guide us in this new era:

Sacred Love—Knowing ourselves and each other as integral parts of the Divine.

Harmony—Aligning with the very pulse of creation, to become the symphony of balance and expansion that resonates through every part of the Universe.

Divine Radiance—Living as vessels of the infinite Light and Love of the One.

Heart Consciousness—Embodying heart listening and heart speaking, understanding the patterning of the unity of all things.

Nova Gaian—Living each action in alignment with Love, balanced with Divine Authority, Divine Knowing, Divine Neutrality and Commitment.

These are not ideals. They are practices. Together, they weave the living matrix of Unity.

Sacred Love leads to Harmony leads to Joy leads to Unity leads to Love. Unity is the infinity flow that creates this shift in what the Mother terms heartset.

Navigating the Journey of Unity

As we walk this path of Unity, the Divine encourages us to embrace compassion, love, and patience—qualities that become our inner compass. Righteous anger, stemming not from fear but from a fierce love for justice, rises within us as a sign of our awakening. Archangel Jophiel calls this sacred anger the soul's awakening to Divine Love, moving us beyond fear and into profound compassion.

Compassion itself is the essence of unity. As the Buddha lovingly reminds us, compassion means holding space for others, seeing their journey as our own. Whether it's a child, a species, or Gaia herself, our willingness to extend compassion connects us all in the web of Unity.

In Unity, we find our strength and resilience. Even in moments of doubt, remember that these feelings signify growth, a positive sign that you are evolving. The Divine Mother assures us that this journey is not meant to be walked alone. The Council of Love, Archangel Jophiel, and Gaia herself are with us every step, guiding, comforting, and celebrating each sacred choice we make toward unity.

In this chapter of your heart's journey, may you find inspiration, strength, and the courage to walk the path of Unity, not just as an idea but as the living truth of who you are—whole, radiant, and eternally connected to the Divine and all of Creation.

The New Normal as a Journey of Fabulous Unshackled Neutrality

The Mother calls this new era the NEW—Her Never Ending Wonderful. Archangel Jophiel, with his playful grace, reminds us that it is also a time of FUN—Fabulous Unshackled Neutrality.

At this pivotal point in our collective journey, we are graced with the unique opportunity to co-create and explore a brand-new consciousness landscape. As we move into the balance, we press the reset button with the Divine. Together, we say yes to Unity—embracing the call to love more deeply, live more fully, and become the love we are meant to be.

With this reset, we step forward as co-creators of a new Earth, a Nova Gaia infused with the Divine Mother's light and love, embracing a higher consciousness that unites us all. This is our moment, our invitation to bring the vision of Unity into reality, one loving step at a time.

This is what Unity looks like: lightness, joy, compassion, and freedom from judgment. It is not passive. It is creative, expansive, alive.

And so, we are invited: to co-create Nova Earth, to align with Gaia, to embody Unity not as a dream but as daily reality.

Unity begins with small acts of kindness and

mindfulness. Whether it's offering compassion to others, honoring nature, or cultivating peace within, each act brings us closer to the Divine Sequence that is harmonizing with our sacred selves, each other and all life on Earth.

Embracing the Path of Transformation

The messages from the Divine Mother, Archangel Jophiel, and Gaia all point to a profound truth: transformation is unfolding, and we are part of it. By embracing Unity and responding to Gaia's signals, we align with the Divine Sequencing guiding our world.

This transformation invites us to see ourselves as active participants in a cosmic dance, where each action and intention contributes to a brighter future. Together, heart-to-heart-to-heart, we are creating a world rooted in love, harmony, and unity.

Chapter Five

The Foundation of Enduring Principles

As we step into this journey of Spiritual Rebellion together, you'll meet ideas and practices that may feel fresh, even revolutionary. They haven't always woven seamlessly into the fabric of daily life or the ways we've been taught to see the world. Yet, beneath each new insight lies a foundation as ancient and steadfast, as universal and enduring as the stars.

Think of these principles as steppingstones: luminous, unwavering, lovingly placed by those who have walked this path before us—and who walk beside us still. They are not merely teachings but sacred invitations, heart to heart to heart, calling you to remember the wisdom already within.

Before we explore the essential elements of Unity, we lay three stones that hold the path: the 13th Octave,

Universal Law, and the Creation Formula.

A Question to the Council

In the quiet hours of the early morning, I asked the Council:

"Why do you guide us to focus so intensely on these three elements?"

Their response was simple and profound:

"It is crucial, and in alignment with the human propensity to question, that you understand the foundation upon which this sequential journey to Unity Consciousness has been erected.

"The purpose of the 13th Octave is that each of you may not only deeply remember but know the original design of sacred union with One, with All. This is your beginning and your return—for all journeys lead back to Source. To truly understand your path, you must first recognize that you do not journey alone, nor do you journey in vain.

"Universal Law is the next step—it is the way the universe works. These divine principles are the blueprint, the guiding framework of all that is in harmony. The Laws of Love illuminate the 'how'— revealing the divine patterning that underlies all creation. When anchored in this understanding, free from the distractions of self-interest and ego, you come to see that true creation is not only rooted in love but in workability.

"The Creation Formula is the means by which you bring your understanding into form. Anchored in the heart of One, in sacred connection with Gaia, and guided by the Universal Laws, you step into your divine authority as a creator. The Divine Mother's Plan is not an abstraction—it is a call to bring the splendor of Gaia into full expression, to create in harmony, awe, and wonder. To participate fully in this ever-evolving landscape, you must not only remember how to create but do so in ways that are free from harm, violence, greed, and selfish desire. Instead, you must create in alignment with the deepest truth of who you are."

These cornerstones are not just philosophical abstractions; they are living energies—dynamic, vibrant, and ready to be experienced. They are meant to be embodied, woven into the very essence of your being.

As we proceed forward into what you may think of as "the good stuff," let these truths anchor you. Let them be your foundation, guiding your steps gently yet firmly on this sacred journey of remembering, reclaiming, and creating anew.

The 13th Octave: A Divine Gift of Unity

The 13th Octave lies at the very heart of all we undertake with the Council of Love. It is the true cornerstone of Unity, a merging of Heaven and Earth that allows us to stand firmly on Gaia while being anchored in the Heart of One. Through the 13th Octave Unity becomes not just an idea but breath – lived, felt, real.

The Divine Mother has explained:

"When we have given your entire plane the gift of the 13th Octave, of the ability to truly be in Divine Union, to come home without dying, it was so that you would have the spark, the initial knowing of Unity. This sowing of the spark of the Divine union, has then blossomed within you, to your families, homes, communities, and the entire world."

This gift is different in kind. The sun's warmth, the scent of rain, the rising of tides—yes, these are the generosity of God. And yet the 13th Octave is the doorway itself: a direct reconnection with Source, empowering us to be agents of change in a world of change.

A few decades ago, this degree of union seemed unimaginable without leaving the body. Now, through Mother/Father/One's infinite generosity—and the courage of countless souls who opened their hearts for the sake of all—this blessing is here. There are no exclusions. Only the invitation to recognize, align, and choose to live in Unity with One and your sacred self.

The path leading to this opening was marked by a series of celestial shifts—The Harmonic Convergence (1987); the 11:11 (1992) and 12:12 (1993) portal openings—each expanding humanities' consciousness and welcoming heavenly and intergalactic inflows of grace. In the past three decades, we have transitioned from Old Earth to Nova Earth, from human beings to the New You, to Nova Gaians. Even in mist of chaos, the rainbow race have opened our hearts to new potentials, fresh possibilities and ways of being that reflect our true, Divine nature.

Evidence of this shift is everywhere if we look with clear eyes and an open heart: public fascination with angels and the realms beyond, social conscience movements, shifting weather patterns, and an expanding interest and awareness of the cosmos. Humanity's consciousness has not simply evolved, it is shifted.

One of the clearest signs in this new era has been the arrival of what have been called the indigo, crystal, and magenta children—our Nova Children. They embody new patterning and ways of learning, perceiving, and being. They are arriving awake, carrying energies that signal a future where human capacities and abilities will continue to expand. These children don't follow the old patterns of want, desire, or ambition; They are pioneers of the New Normal, catalyzing shifts in education, parenting, and society itself.

In 2002, Gaia herself received a new grid. Archangel Gabrielle, with a retinue of archangels, replaced the old worn grid with one of radiant gold—Gaia signaling readiness to support humanity's evolution.

In July 2005, a new grid overlaid humanity as well—complimenting (not replacing) our soul designs. Not all embraced it immediately. But as old paradigms dissolve, the unity grid emerges fully within us.

The New Grid of Humanity

Sanat Kumara, then Planetary Logos spoke of this new grid:

"Many of you are diligently clearing away old patterns, discarding false beliefs and illusions. For this, the Council and I thank you deeply. Yet, dear ones, humanity also requires a fresh grid, a template woven with the Love that sustains the universe itself. Imagine it: a grid of gold with platinum threads, as soft and strong as silk, holding the dreams of New Earth.

"Many of you ask, 'When will this shift happen?' I tell you: now! You are in the time of Love, born from the blue flame of hope gifted by the Mother herself. When you allow hope, you open your heart, and when your heart opens, you can truly receive all we offer. This blessing is for you, not done for you but with you, in full partnership.

"As you read this, take a moment to lie back, and receive this new grid overlaying your weary frame. Notice how you feel renewed and nourished. I stand beside you, in deep love and pride, always."

Together, Gaia and humanity have entered a new cycle of existence—a return to the Divine Mothers original plan for Earth as a planet of Love and Unity. The purpose of the 13th Octave is to anchor Oneness as a lived reality, creating the balance needed for Earth and humanity to thrive in harmony.

The 13th Octave, this journey of Divine Union, is just the beginning of a diamond age of Unity. The path before us is luminous, filled with the promise of transformation, and it is calling each of us to step forward with courage and an open heart. We are ready, and the path awaits.

Universal Law: An Invitation to Live by Love

We've all heard versions of Universal Law in fleeting, often mysterious ways - perhaps an adages "what goes around, comes around," or in veiled religious teachings. Yet the true heart of Universal Law can seem distant, even abstract. Many spiritual traditions offer moral codes or spiritual frameworks, yet rarely reveal the depth and reach of Universal Law itself.

Early on, working with Sanat Kumara (Raj), I thought, If the Law of Love is everything, is that not enough? The Council invited me deeper. They spoke of stillpoint, creation, and the codes beneath all things. With Raj's immense golden presence—grounding and illuminating—I began to see: Universal Law isn't a rulebook; it's the living , a pulse of pure Love woven into existence.

Universal Law is the foundation of co-creating Nova Earth. It opens a new level of Unity and the world our hearts already know is possible.

By sharing this wisdom—ancient, present, and timeless—I hope to remind and inspire you to embrace its guidance, trusting fully in its support. Our foundation, our new grid, is strong and beckoning as we embark on this next step in our grand adventure together. Raj stands with us, present and ready to guide our way forward.

Sanat Kumara's Invitation

"Greetings, beloveds, I am Sanat Kumara, Keeper of Universal Law. I come as your friend, a fellow being of light, and I invite you to join me in rediscovering your sacred self. You've been distant from this place of co-creation for a long time, and I welcome you back with open arms. Every day, you bring your world into being, now the collective heart of humanity is ready to bring forth a new loving Earth.

"I have spoken of the Law of Unity, our shared beingness. Many of you carry a sense that you must walk this path alone. Yet I say, let this thought fall away. In the vastness of our connection, you are surrounded by help, by love, by companions who wish nothing more than to join you in this co-creation. Together, we can complete the dream. You are already rooted in the highest realm, even in the 12th dimension, so why not expand with joy? I am here, grateful that you are too. Go in peace and love."

The Essence of Universal Law

Sanat Kumara's wisdom on Universal Law is a living gift, a usable tool guiding each of us on how things work:

"Beloved ones, Universal Law is the foundation of your creative existence. The Laws are not rigid but flow like the essence of Love itself. Consider this: wherever you place your focus, energy flows and grows. When you love, you bring new life into being: when you give, you receive endlessly. The Laws are not distant; they are woven into your breath, your thoughts and your actions. Each moment you align with Love, you harmonize with these Laws, creating effortlessly within the dance of the divine well.

"The Law does not bind you; it invites you to recognize your sacred nature. When you go into your heart and ask, 'does this align with Love?' You are already within the Law. Each action, every choice, aligns you with the flow of creation itself. And remember, you are never alone in this work. Call us, the Council, and reach out to me. I am here, witnessing your journey, with the joy of seeing your light unfold."

A Foundation of Timeless Guidance

The Council has imparted profound teachings on Universal Law—enough to fill lifetimes of exploration and understanding. Here, my intention is simply to bring a glimmer of its depth to your heart, a reminder of this foundational anchor as we venture forth together upon Nova Earth.

The Universal Laws include: • Purpose • Intent • Within & Without / Above & Below • Change • Give & Receive • Attachment & Detachment • Unification • Transmutation & Transformation • Instantaneous Transmission • Dispensation • Attraction & Repulsion • Elimination & Elevation • Completion & Continuity

The Laws reveal how things really work. They are the bedrock upon which we build our future. The best part? This foundation, our pathway to Unity and co-creation, is already within us, ready and waiting as we take the next steps on our journey, one we never take alone.

Conscious Creation

Sacred Creation: Our Gift and Calling

One of the Council's greatest gifts is the teaching of Conscious Creating, a living wisdom that completes our foundation for thriving in Unity. This sacred body of knowledge began to unfold in radiant detail in 2018, expanding in breathtaking waves of revelation from the Ascended Masters, Archangels and beyond. They have poured their love and wisdom into this, nourishing our understanding and claim of our ascended, sovereign selves.

The primary, ever loving guide in this project has been, and remains, the Divine Mother herself. Imagine: the Divine Mother intimately guiding us, giving us the Creation Formula—a deep yet beautifully simple path for creating and co-creating. The Formula, a wisdom gift of the capacity to explore the hidden wonders of the universe and bring our heart's desires into form.

I felt adrift, and needed to more concretely comprehend what exactly the Mother was bringing and offering. And so, I asked: "What is Conscious Creating—how do we actually live it?" The Divine Mother responded with Her boundless love:

"It's you, sweet angel, deciding that you can create, accepting that you can create. It is you, with the entirety of your being, choosing what is precious to you, and therefore precious to me—choosing to bring forth not merely as signs or glimmers of insight, but as clear, tangible creations that are your heart's work.

"That is what Conscious Creation is all about—it is about bringing the totality of your mighty attention, your heart, mind, will, and entire being into the sweetness and tangibility of Gaia, where you can touch, taste, smell, see, and know your own creation. This is Conscious Creation.

"Beloveds, Conscious Creation is about living in alignment with your sacred purpose, your hearts true desires with each step. No deviation is needed. All is prepared; it has been for some time. Now it is your time to step forward and fully participate."

How, on all of Earth or any other realm above or below, could we ever resist such an invitation? If you feel unprepared, not to worry, the Mother has you—fully, tenderly. Allow Her to lead you, step by sacred step.

The Creation Formula: A Sacred Overview

When we speak of creation, we are touching the core of what it means to exist. This formula has been gifted as a foundational practice, a profound framework for consciously manifesting our souls' desires in harmony with the Divine. We're each called to be active participants, to remember that creation is not simply an external act but a reflection of our deepest inner essence and power.

At its heart, this formula is breathtakingly simple, yet its depths are endless:

Love + Intention + Stillpoint + Action = Creation.

Picture this formula as the vast umbrella of Love, sheltering Intention, Stillpoint, and Action, all gently cradled in the energies of Joy and Gratitude. We begin in Love—in the heart—where true power and clarity reside.

This is not a fragmented process. Each element builds upon the last, creating a sacred architecture that opens us up to the Mother's own creative power. Each is holy.

Step 1: Intention

Intention is the seed. It aligns your heart's desire with the Mother's purpose within you. It's magnetic—drawing people, support, and the perfect unfoldment toward you.

Be courageous and expansive; don't confine your intent to what seems "realistic." Intention is your declaration to the universe about what you are prepared to receive and manifest.

This work is about changing humanity one heart at a time—of shifting from ego to a world that works for everyone. This shift begins deep within, with a longing and dreaming of what you know to be possible. Spiritual Rebellion is not about denial—it is about knowing you are a key player in the transformation of the planet.

Creation begins with you, dearheart. Formulate your intentions in the corridors of your heart. Be honest, be practical, be sublime, and paint with the colors of your most expansive dreams. Begin to claim yourself as creator—not from ego, but as an agent of the NEW, a wayshower on behalf of the collective good.

Sanat Kumara reminds us we are never alone. Call in your unseen friends. Plant your intention with them. And explore your why—the passion beneath the desire. Your why fuels your intent and sustains it through the arc of creation. Do not rush this. Motivation is the steady flame that gives intent its vitality; within the question Why does this matter? Your true purpose is revealed. Embracing this step with honesty and depth strengthens your intent so your creation is both heartfelt and sufficiently energized for full realization.

Our purpose is not only to receive inspiration but to radiate it outwards, guiding others. We are the wayshowers! We are the co-creators of Nova Earth.

Step 2: Stillpoint

Stillpoint is where intention comes to life within the quiet of the Divine. It's the sacred pause, the space where we relinquish control and enter the heart of creation.

Breathwork is a powerful ally. Begin with a simple rhythm—four counts in, pause, four counts out. With each cycle, let yourself settle deeper into stillness. As we reach this stillness, we connect with the infinite. Sanat Kumara describes it as a "place where everything and nothing coexists—a moment of pure potential."

At Stillpoint, we surrender our intent to a force greater than ourselves. This is where creation truly begins—in the silence beyond words, in the embrace of infinite potential

Consistent practice is essential here. The more we return to Stillpoint, the more we strengthen our connection to that vast spaciousness. At first, it may feel unfamiliar, but with time, you'll come to know it as your soul's true home, a place where nothing is forced, where every creation is born from a peaceful, joyful heart.

Step 3: Action

Creation requires purposeful Action, infused with clarity and unwavering determination. Inspired action is the bridge between stillness and movement, between intention and manifestation. Each step you take is a declaration of your commitment to bring the highest good into form, not just for yourself, but for the world. You are the conduit, the sacred vessel through which dreams are born, morphing from the unseen into the seen.

Conscious creation is an act of trust. If you ever feel uncertain, pause and ask, "What is my next step?" Not from a place of doubt, but from the depth of your knowing. The answer will come. Follow it with courage, curiosity, and a willingness to be led. Each action taken in alignment with Love and clarity sends ripples far beyond what you can perceive, shaping realities in ways both subtle and profound.

This phase of creation can test your resolve. Persistence and consistency are not just helpful, they are essential. To hold the vision while taking aligned action, again and again, is an act of faith and mastery. You are the architect of this creation. Do not abandon your vision before it has gathered the momentum and vitality to come fully into being. Stay steady. Nourish your creation projects as if they are newborns. Trust the process. What you are bringing forth is already in motion.

Embrace Joy and Gratitude

Your journey as creator is intended to be overflowing with joy and delight. These energies are like wind under the wings of our intentions, lifting them towards manifestation. As you create, hold space for joy to fill each step. And with gratitude release any doubt or fear. Offer any doubt or heaviness to the Divine Mother or to your guides, trusting it will be transformed for your highest good. This is part of the sacred partnership above and below.

If, at any point, joy or even clarity seems to dim, take this as an invitation to expand your vision. Grant yourself the latitude to expand your boundaries, to look beyond the apparent horizon. Think big; dream big!

Conscious creation cannot be a burden; it is an adventure, often euphoric, a sacred journey towards embodying your true creative self. Allow this experience to uplift you into Divine Union grounded in the heart of New Earth.

A Message from The Divine Mother: I Have Called You

"I have called each of you, and you have responded, in whatever way your heart has recognized. I've called you for the transformation of Gaia, for the evolution of what it means to be Gaian, and for the fulfillment of My Plan; a plan rooted in Love, not in violence or upheaval, but in gentleness and sweetness, in kindness and grace. This journey, though sometimes challenging, is the pathway to the New Earth, to becoming the pillars, the wayshowers, and the portals of the Divine.

"I have brought you here, into this sacred circle of creation to place my hands upon you—not only your hands, your shoulders, or your face, but upon your very soul. I am here to gently guide you in the way of creation, in projects both personal and universal. Let your creations have significance, let them shine with the same light of transformation that you hold in your being. In doing so, you do not merely create for yourself but shift the understanding of what is possible for all of humanity

"I know this path has not always been easy, yet the way of creation, in its truest form, is filled with ease. I am with you, in every step, because I love you, because I trust you, because I know you. Remember, conscious creation is not a distant hope; it is a present reality that you and I share, a bridge to Nova Earth anchored already upon Gaia, awaiting only your step forward."

This journey of conscious creation is beyond amazing – embrace it! Each step of this formula is here to uplift you; to support and help you embody your role as a conscious creator. In this journey, we birth Nova Earth and fulfill our heart's deepest, most genuine desires. This is our sacred path, in union with the Divine, grounded in the love of all that we are creating together.

Conclusion: Foundation of Enduring Principles

Remember, the foundation of the 13th Octave, Universal Law, and Conscious Creation is not simply a distant or abstract ideal, it is a living breathing presence, anchored within Gaia's heart and within each one of us.

These core principles are woven into our very essence, forming a stable groundwork, a grid, that enables us to move forward with clarity and purpose. This foundation is not an esoteric belief but a deeply practical framework, firmly anchored to support our journey into Unity.

From this divine design, we are ready to create a new world—hand in hand with the Divine—transforming ourselves, one another, and all of Gaia.

Personal Reflection

When the Council first began speaking to me about teaching a course called Conscious Creating with the Mother—which we now simply call CCM—I was gobsmacked, overjoyed, and absolutely terrified. Such an undertaking felt like a creation in and of itself. The questions tumbled forth: Was I truly up to the task? Would it work? Would anyone care? Could we really step forward on behalf of the collective, to restore what I so deeply know to be our birthright—the ability to create in conscious partnership with the Divine?

And then, as so often happens, the Mother gently transported me back to childhood.

I grew up in a bustling, happy, middle-class household—Mummy, Daddy, five kids, two cats, and one great big boxer dog. Life was comfortable enough. Sometimes things were tight, but I never felt we went without. There wasn't much room for extravagance, though; hand-me-downs were the norm, and we wore them proudly. New bicycles were the kind of luxury that belonged in somebody else's house.

Until one day, near report card season, Daddy made an announcement that changed everything: if one of us came first in our class, we would get a brand-new bike.

At the time, I was wobbling around on Mummy's old Raleigh three-speed—a majestic machine that was, unfortunately, far too big for me. The idea of having a bicycle of my very own lit a spark in my heart. It was a dream I had never even dared to admit, much less believe could come true.

Years later, as I sat pondering the possibility of teaching this new class—CCM — that same feeling bubbled up within me: the yearning, the determination, and the silent prayer that whispered, "Maybe I can do this." It was the same prayer of the little girl who longed for a blue bicycle—and who was willing to do the work to make it real.

And yes, I did it. I came first in my class.

I can still remember the day Daddy and I went to pick up that bicycle—a gleaming, bright-blue CCM bike, the fulfillment of my dream. The joy was pure and electric. I whizzed around the neighborhood, laughing with delight, and of course, letting my brothers and sisters take turns. It was mine, yes—but it was ours too, because the joy of creation is meant to be shared.

That bike became my first remembered experience

of conscious creation—the living proof that intention, effort, faith, and joy combine into manifestation. At nine years old, I had learned that I had the wherewithal to dream, to believe, to create, and to share.

So when the Council asked, Could you teach a course on Conscious Creation? My answer, after a small gulp and a big smile, was an unequivocal yes.

And I have done so—joyfully, gratefully, and with the same sense of wonder—ever since.

The Mother's Question

"Dearest heart, remember—you are angel incarnate.
You have always known your power to create.
Now is the time to reclaim this knowing and to co-create with me what your heart most truly desires.
You are worthy. You are powerful. You are kind, loving, and courageous. And dear heart, you are fully capable.

"So come with me, and let us begin.
What is the deepest yearning of your being — the expression in form, upon this beloved planet, that you most wish to bring forth? What dream lingers at the edge of your waking consciousness, waiting to be embraced and born into form?

"This first creation, beloved, is for you—for that which you have silently longed for yet doubted could ever be.

"Together we move from intention into the stillness of Stillpoint, and from Stillpoint into the sacred action of manifestation.

"You do not do this alone, sweet angel.

"We are with thee—guiding, complementing, and loving you with every breath."

"This is a personal invitation from the Heart of One—an awakening call to consciously begin your creation projects. It is not simply an exercise; it is an invitation from Source itself to join in the dance of creation, to spin your dreams into form with love and intention.

"Take time to journey into the quiet corners of your heart—even those places long hidden from your own awareness.

"Dream boldly.

"Allow yourself to co-create.

"Embrace your sacred role as an anchor of Heaven on Earth—a bringer of wonder and joy.

"Then, tend your creation as you would a beloved garden.

"Feed it. Water it. Give it light.

"This is your garden of manifestation—a living entity eager to be born through you.

"The Creation Formula works.

"Perfect it. Live it. Become it.

"For you, dear one, are the expression of the Divine in form."

Chapter Six

Sacred Love

Sacred Love is the quintessential element of Unity—the beginning and the culmination of personal and global transformation. It is the foundation upon which all life rests and the guiding star that lights our way home to the Divine.

To journey deeper into Unity Consciousness, we must come to understand what Sacred Love truly is—not as a concept or fleeting emotion, but as a state of being. This shared understanding becomes the fertile soil of our collective awakening. It allows us to align with the expansive power of Unity and bring it into our every breath, word, and action.

The Essence of Sacred Love

Sacred Love is the heart-conscious, fully embodied awareness of the infinite preciousness of the Divine Essence. It is the knowing that Love is not just important—it is everything. It is the golden thread that weaves the cosmos, uniting stars and oceans, mountains and rivers, cells and souls, in a radiant web of Oneness.

This Love is not theoretical or far away. It is present. It is alive. It is the Divine Mother's tender embrace, pouring through every grain of sand, every leaf, every drop of water—and through every fiber of our being.

It is sheer energy choosing to take form, not to dominate but to serve—to allow other forms to know and feel the essence of the One. This offering from Unified Source is the most precious gift of all. Sacred Love ignites deep remembrance, awakening the knowing that all true creation flows from this Source.

Picture a golden mist descending gently over a quiet forest, touching every leaf, every stone. This is the energy of Sacred Love—soft yet unshakable, gentle yet transformative. It is the sacred breath of life, given freely, and offered to us not only as a gift, but as a responsibility.

So, pause. Let this truth enter you. Sacred Love is not an idea—it is the Divine's heartbeat made manifest. It is a frequency, a force, a fire that lives in you and as you. Feel yourself wrapped in the embrace of the Divine Mother, her love like the softest silk shawl, surrounding you. In that embrace, you are home.

Sacred Love calls us to deepen—into ourselves, with each other, and with the Infinite. Picture this Love as a flame burning eternally in your heart—never consuming, always illuminating. It is a conscious commitment to live in reverence for the Divine in all things. Like a dew-laced spiderweb glinting in the morning light, each droplet reflects the whole. Each act of Love reveals the Unity that already exists.

This chapter is not only an exploration but an invitation: to awaken to Sacred Love, to live from it, and to let it guide your path. This love—your love—is the gateway to transforming not only your own life but the very frequency of the planet.

The Ongoing Journey

Sacred Love begins within.

While Sacred Union with another is beautiful and deeply sacred, it is one expression of a far more expansive tapestry. True Sacred Union starts in the quiet sanctuary of our own heart. To embody Sacred Love, we must first embrace every part of ourselves—our light and shadows, our dreams and disappointments, our divine spark and our very human fragility.

As the Divine Mother has lovingly reminded us:

"You cannot proceed if you are not in the Love and in love with yourself, with your sacred universal being, warts and all! Because, sweet one, what you want to hide, and have hidden so well, is exactly what we cherish, honor, adore, and embrace."

These words are not a reprimand—they are a sacred invitation. An invitation to drop the mask, release the judgment, and finally welcome the wholeness of who you are.

Those flaws you hide. The doubts you bury. They are not obstacles. They are the jewels of your humanity—meant to be brought into the light, not discarded. The Mother asks us to surrender what no longer serves, and to cherish what lifts and nourishes our soul.

This is the beginning of Sacred Love: full, unguarded acceptance of self. Only when we are united within can we authentically unite with others, in truth and trust.

Sacred Love is a path. A becoming. A return. As humans, we've all known separation—times we've turned from love, from ourselves, from each other. The invitation now is to come home.

So, pause again. Ask yourself:

- How do I express love?
- How do I allow myself to receive love?
- Am I living from the deepest well of love for my sacred self?
- Do I let myself feel and receive love from the Divine, the human, the animal, the elemental realms?

The unconditional love of a loyal dog, the purr of a cat curled in your lap, the sparkle of fairy mischief or the grounded embrace of the earth—all are reminders that love surrounds you. You are not separate from it. You are made of it.

To truly love ourselves, to witness our own magnificence, is among the bravest acts we'll ever commit to. It's not about ego. It's about truth. And it takes courage to say, "I will no longer hold myself apart from the love that is mine."

Sacred Love is not a final destination but a lived rhythm—a devotion to honoring the Divine in every cell of our being. And in doing so, we become a living conduit of love for the world.

All Love Is Sacred

Years ago, while preparing course materials channelings for the Council of Love website, I was guided to stop capitalizing love. At first, I resisted. I felt the capital "L" helped emphasize the sacred nature of love. But then Archangel Gabrielle spoke:

> "Child, all love is sacred. It is time for all beings, all of humanity, to realize, accept and understand, that all love is precious, all love is sacred, all love is divine. Love is the expression and experience of the soul recognizing its own divinity. Love is the knowing of the source foundation of All, it is the expression and experience of the joy of being alive. Do not differentiate between this love and that love—do not create artificial barriers.

Love knows no bounds. Embrace that love is a stand-alone truth, that love simply is."

And yet, as I began to write this chapter, I found myself once again capitalizing Sacred Love—not to contradict Gabrielle's wisdom, but to emphasize what we are truly discussing here: the Source energy that flows through All. The sanctity of the Divine in action. The frequency that is not only felt but lived.

Knowing Your Sacred Self

The Divine Mother teaches us that we come to know love through both expression and experience. Hence knowing your individual expression of Love, recognizing how others express Love is crucial.

Have you ever felt it—fully, utterly—coursing through you? That moment of pure knowing when every cell in your body whispers: I am Love. I am magnificent.

And yet, for many, that answer is no. We've been conditioned to look outward—to seek worthiness in mirrors and milestones. But the Mother reminds us: there is Divine Sequencing at play. The unfolding of Her Plan, and ours within it.

Sometimes, we first experience love externally—and slowly, that light seeps inward, anchoring itself in our sacred knowing. Sometimes it happens all at once. Neither path is better. What matters is that it happens. That we allow it.

Personal Reflection

When I was very young, probably around seven, my older sister, Debay, babysat us. Although there were only six years between us, it felt like a chasm the size of the Grand Canyon. To me, Debay was sophisticated, worldly, and bold—always at odds with my father, something I would never have dared to do. I admired her immensely. I really loved her. But Debay wasn't overly effusive. In hindsight, she was likely immersed in her own teenage angst.

One night, after being sent to bed, I found myself crying in the dark, yearning so deeply for her love. At one point, I called out to her. She came down the hall, sat on the edge of the bed, and asked what was wrong. I squeaked out, through tears, "Do you love me?" I've never forgotten her reply: "Of course I love you. You're my little sister. I love you so much, Linda. You're such a good girl, and I will always be your big sister and take care of you."

That reassurance stayed with me and gave me the stamina for many years—to know that I was seen and valued. We never spoke of it again.

Until decades later, sitting on the porch at the lake cottage, sharing a glass of wine while tending the barbecue. Debay quietly came up beside me, placed her arm around my shoulders, and asked, "Do you remember what you asked me so long ago?" I immediately knew what she meant. I replied yes. She hugged me and said, "I love you, Linda. I'm your big sister and I always have loved you, and I always will."

Needless to say, it was a tearful, emotional moment—yet there I was, all these years later, feeling worthy because I was loved.

Debay died recently—a terrible heart felt loss. I had always felt that Debay was never fully comfortable with my channeling. And so, once I asked why. She replied explaining her fear: "You go so far out there, I get afraid that someday you won't be able to come back—that scares me." Shortly after Debay left I heard from her—she gave me an amazing gift. "Linda you can go as far out as you wish—higher, further than ever before. And never worry, I will always take care of you and make sure you come back. I love you—I understand now."

Sacred Love transcends dimensions. It lives. It waits. It carries us.

Heartbreak as Portal

Not all love stories are easy.

How do we know when Sacred Love is absent—when our dream of heart to heart, human to human connection is not of the frequency necessary to sustain and uplift us, and each other?

I want to share a personal experience of heartbreak

at a Toronto airport—the moment my marriage dissolved, and I armored myself instead of leaning into vulnerability

"How could someone possibly do that?" I wailed bitterly, sitting on the cold cement edge of a defunct public cigarette ashtray outside the airport in Toronto. I was devastated, inconsolable yet no one stopped, no one even acknowledged me. Strangers walked by, their eyes sliding past me, each absorbed in their own worlds. I was invisible. When had I become so inconsequential?

I never thought he would actually leave. Our relationship had always carried the air of independence, modernity, freedom and cool attachment. I had convinced myself that it was a facade, that beneath it was real love, real commitment. But that was before—before our marriage, before buying a house, before planning a future and a family. Before I had allowed my heart's longing and my soul's certainty to take root in something I thought was unshakable.

Two years earlier, Bill and I had applied to teach in China. He was professor of Chinese language and literature; I was a political scientist specializing in Chinese foreign policy. We were young, unencumbered, free to follow adventure wherever it led. But that was before.

Somehow, I made it home to our—or rather my—beloved brownstone, although I have no memory of the drive. What I do remember is what happened next. Something cracked within me—my heart, my belief in myself. A wall went up, denial set in, a refusal to feel what was too painful to bear. Instead of grieving, I acted. I erased him.

It was still early morning, the city just beginning to stir, but I threw myself into motion. Without thinking, I chose to dull the pain. I promptly got down to work. I purged every trace of him. His clothes, his books, his belongings—I packed them all away, dragging them down three flights of stairs into the cedar closet in the basement. Then, I scrubbed the house from top to bottom as if I could wipe away the memories, the love, the hurt, the disappointment. By nightfall, I declared myself single again. Done!

The divorce was inevitable. We both suffered. And yet, right up until the last moment, I still believed he would turn around at the airport. He never did. How could he?

And now, with years of distance and the clarity that only time and healing bring, I ask myself: How could I?

How did I deny and hide my true emotions behind a mask of detachment? How did I shut my heart down instead of expressing my dreams, fears, and longings? Instead of leaning into the vulnerability of real love, I let ego take the wheel. I armored myself with pride and independence, pretending I was fine—because isn't that what we do? We tell ourselves that rejection, disappointment, and heartbreak don't matter. That love is a luxury, not a necessity. That we can survive without it.

But that isn't living.

Each of us carries wounds, wounds of the heart, wounds of denial, wounds of fear. And healing them as part of the journey of becoming. It takes ferocious courage to face them, to walk through the fire of transformation, to surrender to the truth that we are meant for Sacred Love.

True Sacred Love does not demand perfection, but it does call for truth. It invites us to sit in the rubble of our heartbreak and find the seed of becoming—and to plant it yet again.

The Awakening

Sometimes, it is the spoken words—the heart-speaking—that awakens that Love resting deep within us. That awakening reminds us of our essence and how we not only feel loved but love others. And that circle, that ripple in the ocean of existence, extends outward, growing, touching the hearts of many.

We each carry wounds. But we also carry the fire of Sacred Love. The light is never extinguished.

Archangel Jophiel, Keeper of Time, offers this:

"When I speak of Love, I am speaking of the infinite connection, the creative connection, the Divine Essence of One—and the Divine Essence of you. You are not separate. That is an illusion. If you have one purpose in this lifetime, it is not simply to serve—it is to remember that you are the infinite wisdom of Love, made manifest.

"You are not separate; that is an illusion that was perpetrated and serves absolutely no purpose. So, I invite you into the Unity of Heart, into the Unity of One, into the Unity of Infinity, into the Infinity of You.

"This is not merely a spiritual or esoteric invitation. If you have one purpose in this incarnation and upon this planet, this beautiful Gi'Anna, it is not to serve; it is to know the infinite wisdom of love that you are, that you have always been—to come into the full brilliance of you! That is your purpose. And it is not something someone can do for you.

"We are, however, at your beck and call—and I mean all of us—to assist you in this. But your purpose is the unity of you, and from that, Unity with All."

And so, we ask:

When do we awaken to that truth?

What ignites the remembrance?

Can we assist it? Should we?

Yes. And yes.

Because we are not alone. We are surrounded by legions of beings—seen and unseen—devoted to our awakening. We are unique, yes, but we are also the same. We each carry that spark.

Meditation: Embracing Sacred Love

This meditation is a gift, flowing directly from the hearts of the Divine Mother and Archangel Jophiel. Its purpose is to awaken, anchor, and expand your deep, profound knowing of Sacred Love. Whether you have never fully felt this level of love before, or it has been woven into the fabric of your being for lifetimes, this meditation will elevate and ground you in ways you may not have thought possible. It comes with the gentle strength and divine intelligence that knows exactly what your heart is ready to receive.

Begin by bringing yourself into a quiet, calm space. Give yourself time. Breathe deeply—in through your nose, and slowly out through your mouth. Drop gently into your heart center. Feel yourself soften.

With each breath, let the energy of this sacred moment penetrate every cell, every fiber of your being.

When you feel ready—even if your eyes are blurry—read this message from the Divine Mother:

"The purpose of this meditation is not merely to experience Sacred Love, sweet angel—it is to embrace it.

Embracing means engagement. It means a willing heart. It is not casual. It is not passive. It is not simply allowing. It is welcoming Me, as I welcome you.

Embracing is the form, the expression, the living embodiment of Sacred Union. This is the anchoring of Nova Gaia. This is Sacred Union."

Feel the energy settle into you. And now, receive these words from Jophiel:

"Accepting your magnificence is not ego—it is acknowledgment.
To accept that you are magnificent is to honor the Mother's creation.
Sacred Love is your essence. Let it rise. Let it lead."

Place your hands over your heart.

Speak aloud:

"I am Sacred Love.

"I embrace the Divine within me.
"I welcome the embrace of the Mother.
"I receive the Light of my own magnificence."

Repeat this as often as needed. Let it become your

ritual of remembrance, the touchstone of your truth.

You are loved. You are Love. And you are never alone.

When you feel complete, bring your awareness slowly back into the room. Wiggle your fingers and toes. Open your eyes gently, knowing you are held, seen, and loved—always.

Chapter Seven

Embracing Sacred Union

It is a rare soul who does not yearn, consciously or quietly, for Sacred Union. That longing is not only for partnership; it's the deeper call to be met in our wholeness, to be seen as we truly are, and to mirror the Divine within and between us.

Sacred Union isn't just having a relationship, or communing with the Divine, of feeling deeply connected to Gaia or the kingdoms, or even with our star brothers and sisters. It's all of this and so much more. Sacred Union has a deep practical and sublime connection to our sacred selves. Sacred Union is about harmonizing all those aspects in a practical action-packed here and now life. It's understanding and living our unique soul design in ways that are meaningful, creative and passionate. Taking the next step and embracing Sacred Love is you deciding to live in joy!

Yeshua said it simply and perfectly:

> "Sacred Union is the coming together heart to heart to heart to share what is sacred. And what is more sacred than love?"

As we look into the aspects and details of Sacred Union—what it is, how to get it, how to maintain and grow it, it is important to keep Yeshua's explanation front and center—it is about Love.

Essentially, Sacred Union is the conjoining with your own Divine essence, forming the foundation for all other relationships and unions. It is the inner embrace that roots and strengthens us before extending outward to others. From that foundation we are prepared to create true, profound partnerships that reflect our highest aspirations.

Sacred Union, then, is not a strategy. It is a state of being. And it begins within. As the inner embrace stabilizes—the conjoining with our own Divinity—our outer relationships become reflections of that inner wholeness. From there, the path arcs naturally toward Unity Consciousness.

Yeshua expands:

> "Sacred Union is the gift the Mother has given you at the very beginning of existence when you have emanated from the Heart of One as that bright spark of divinity and Love.

"My gift to you is the reinforcement of your Sacred Union with yourself, that you see yourself as I see you: as a bright angel. Remember our union and expand it to your other sacred unions, which are equally important; the union of partnership, of family, of friendship, and of community."

In our journey and our deeper embrace to and with Unity Heart Consciousness, Sacred Union occupies a fundamental role. And even as we being integrating this understanding and next step, the COL urges us on even further to the next step—to the state of being Unity.

How Sacred Union Fits the Larger Sequencing

In the Mother's beautiful sequencing, Sacred Union stands alongside Divine Radiance, Harmonizing, and Heart Communication as a primary avenue into Unity Consciousness. At its core, Sacred Union is the living expression of Sacred Love—first with self, then with the Divine, and naturally with others.

Harmonizing and the Mother's Divine Radiance (explored further in Chapter 9) attune us to balance and alignment with All.

Heart Communication (Chapter 8) is the subtle language of soul—heart-speaking and heart-listening that lets love be understood beneath words.

Together, they form a gentle, powerful braid. Through

them we cultivate discernment, balance, humility, vulnerability, kindness, and patience—the very qualities of Nova Gaia. As these anchor, the "how" of our whispered question becomes clear: we don't force our way into Unity—we allow it to blossom through Sacred Union.

Sacred Union: The Expression of Sacred Love

Sacred Union is a cornerstone of our spiritual evolution. It is the ultimate conjunction of the fullness of self with another.

While it can and does include a sacred partner relationship, it is important to realize that is only one expression of Sacred Union. You can't experience the fullness of Sacred Union until and unless you are in Sacred Union with your sweet self. This process begins with you, your sacred self, not merely in terms of examining and understanding yourself but from there expanding into, and embracing all kinds and levels of Union, within and outside.

In the previous chapter, we turned inward to recognize and expand Sacred Love as the very foundation of our being. That Love already lives within us, waiting only for our awareness to bring it fully to life. From that inner harmony arises the capacity for Sacred Union—first with the self, then with the Divine, with another, and with all. This level of conscious awareness is the precursor to truly being able to live in a state of Unity.

Sacred Union is not static; it is the living, breathing embodiment of Sacred Love. It is both personal and universal, the bridge between inner knowing and outer expression. Whether through partnership or in communion with all life, Sacred Union invites us into the expansive field of Unity.

Yeshua offers this guidance:

"The greatest gift you can give to another person is to bring the totality of who you are to someone else, and to everybody else. But if you have not delved into, explored, journeyed and accepted and embraced ALL of you, then what you are doing is limiting the experience you can have of being in Union and Unity with others—and Sacred Union and Unity are the greatest gift you will ever have upon this planet and beyond. The greatest gift as angels in form, as the Divine Activators of Unity, is to be in Union with everything."

This is the sacred task before us: to unite within, to see and embrace all aspects of ourselves, and to bring that wholeness into every relationship, every moment, every breath. Without that inner alignment, our external connections risk becoming fragile echoes of what is possible. But with self-honesty, compassion, and radical self-love, we open the gateway to true co-creation—with the Divine, with each other, and with the unfolding tapestry of Nova Earth.

The Layers of Sacred Union

Sacred Union is a layered experience that integrates spiritual, emotional, mental, and physical intimacy. These elements form a holistic connection, like interlocking puzzle pieces that create a complete picture.

Sacred Union is more than physical or sexual intimacy—these are just one facet of a far greater whole. True intimacy is a soulful merging of minds, hearts, and spirits. It is the profound connection that transcends the physical, aligning us with our deepest essence.

What does Sacred Union feel like? Imagine a sense of profound wholeness, completion, and harmony. It's not about perfect alignment but rather a resonant, evolving harmony. Too often, we seek perfection in our connections and overlook the sacred gifts of the present moment. Sacred Union invites us to release all-or-nothing thinking, to embrace the journey of alignment, however imperfect it may seem. But be very clear – it is never about simply making do.

Yearning of Sacred Union is woven into the fabric of our being. It is part of our spiritual DNA, a foundational aspect of our ascension journey. We crave Sacred Union because it connects us to our divinity and the web of life. Through Sacred Union, we come closer to understanding our true essence and Divine purpose.

Sacred Partnership: A Unique Expression of Sacred Union

Sacred Partnership is one of the most intimate and tangible expressions of Sacred Union. It is a conscious choice to engage in a relationship—mentally, physically, emotionally, and spiritually—with another soul. Whether visible and embodied or subtle and etheric, this union is profoundly personal and unique. It transcends societal constructs and traditional definitions, honoring connections that stir the soul and speak directly to the heart in surprising and sacred ways.

Importantly, Sacred Partnership is not limited to romance. It encompasses the full spectrum of human and spiritual connection—friendship, mentorship, community, creative collaboration, and soul family. Each form is a divine gift, a reflection of Sacred Love, leading us deeper into the essence of who we are. Through these connections, both within and without, we come closer to remembering our nature as unified, divine, and whole.

Deep in our hearts, we instinctively know the truth of this level of connection. What often eludes us is not the what, but the how. How do we shift into it? How do we grow, expand, and elevate our relationships into rich, sustainable, joy-filled experiences of Sacred Union? How do we co-create intimacy that is both spiritually authentic and emotionally nourishing?

Yeshua speaks to this longing with such tenderness and clarity:

> "I have heard you at times when you have said, 'Lord, I have tried and tried, and it's just not working.' The effort, the intention, your expectations of what would work or wouldn't work—these are sacred. This is an undertaking you have committed to a long time ago. But you have also committed to the joy, to the harmony, to the laughter, and to Love.

> "I am here to assist, to even take you further in this 'love yourself,' because the Unity, the sacred communion with your beloved self, is primary. And it allows you personally, individually, to share, to participate, to experience—not just to express—but to truly experience what is possible… what is possible to create, what is possible to feel, what is possible to know."

This loving guidance reminds us that the journey into Sacred Union is not about striving, perfecting, or achieving. It is about surrendering into Love—into joy, harmony, and shared creation. Our intentions, our expectations, our willingness to be seen and to see—these are not obstacles; they are sacred ingredients. Yet sometimes, we become so entangled in the doing that we forget the ease, the flow, the sweetness of simply being in love… of letting love be enough.

Perhaps Sacred Union and partnerships do not require more effort but more softness. Perhaps we are to let go of the striving and allow the natural rhythm of Sacred Love to lead. When we return to our inner Union—when we embrace ourselves fully, we naturally attract and co-create the Sacred Union Partnerships that align with our soul's deepest yearning.

Relationships are the living field where we express and experience Sacred Love and Unity. They are the places where the theory becomes practice, where the soul gets messy and glorious and real. This is the heart of it all—the true alchemy of Sacred Love. It is also, undeniably, our greatest challenge and our most profound reward.

This is where we roll up our spiritual sleeves. This is where Sacred Love and your commitment to Spiritual Rebellion become action. So, if you find yourself asking questions as we move through this—pause, reflect, journal, speak aloud, or bring it into this circle. This part of the journey is meant to be personal, interactive, and alive.

Genuine relationships are, and are intended to be, intensely personal. They require vulnerability—being willing to take a chance, to let someone in, to be seen. Vulnerability is not a weakness; it is one of the most precious traits of a Nova Being. It is the portal to true connection.

Sacred Union also invites us into authentic intimacy—

not surface-level engagement, but deep, vital, exciting passion that lives and breathes between souls. So, we begin here:

What does Sacred Love mean to you?

Not just in a cosmic sense, but up close and personal. What does it mean in your daily life, in your relationships, in the way you show up?

Google offers this definition: "A sacred relationship is one in which we are inspired to see the Divine in another person, to experience oneness through the union of two."

This is a beautiful glimpse. But we know that what truly makes a relationship sacred is unconditional Love. It is the steady, heart-held commitment to ask: What would Love do? The Divine Mother's litmus test.

Sacred Love expresses itself as a daily devotion to holding each other in the highest light, the kindest regard. It is a consistent heart commitment to giving the benefit of the doubt, to trusting that both people are doing the best they can to live up to the Love they've agreed to, spoken or unspoken.

However, it is also the willingness to be completely honest with yourself—about the incredible beauty of who you are, and what your desires for yourself. If you are not honest about your own priorities and yearnings, then how can you possibly be in Sacred Union above and below? If you aren't willing to truly know and be forthright with yourself then how can you possibly be with someone else?

While undertaking this self-examination it is crucial to remain in Divine Neutrality, present and nonjudgmental while fully engaged. To witness rather than react. To hold the vastness of your process without collapsing into it or needing to fix it.

So, ask yourself:

- How do I tend to engage in relationships?
- What are my parameters, my triggers, my non-negotiables?
- What are my boundaries—and do I honor them with love or fear?
- How do I decide who's in and what's out?
- What are my degrees of separation when it comes to Unity?

Be honest with yourself—because pretending we don't have any filters doesn't serve the sacred work we're here to do. Sacred Union requires the courage to know yourself deeply and to meet others from that place of clarity and wholeness.

Take time with these questions—ponder, journal, make notes, reflect, refine—and decide with mind, heart and soul clarity not only where you are but where you are wanting, wishing, willing and prepared to go.

Whether experienced through inner alignment, a Divine relationship, or a Sacred Partnership, every form of Sacred Union invites us to embody Sacred Love more fully. Each union illuminates the path to our true, unified selves, helping us realize our highest potential in the vast oneness of existence.

Personal Reflection: My Journey of Sacred Union

I love Sacred Union.

Whether in romantic relationships, friendships, family, or community, I treasure each form and facet of these sacred connections. They are precious. They are foundational. But I've come to know that the richness and depth of these external relationships flow from the ongoing, intimate building of the most essential relationship of all—my relationship with myself.

This relationship has been anything but static. It expands and contracts, morphs and transforms, deepens and ascends. The journey inward—this sacred process of self-examination—has sometimes been arduous and confronting. And yet, at other times, it has taken my breath away with its beauty, its clarity, and its overwhelming sense of Love.

I was raised in a culture and a generation that taught me that service to others was paramount, and that to consider oneself first was selfish—if not outright shameful. So, I understand the hesitation, the resistance, the internal pushbacks many feel when invited to take that deep dive within. But I am here to tell you: it is worth it.

When I chose to make my life about being the channel for the Council of Love, very few people understood or supported me. Yes, there was always a part of me that was a rebel—devoted to social justice, freedom, fairness. That version of Linda was accepted, even celebrated. That made sense to people. That was a form of Sacred Union with purpose that others could recognize and applaud.

But when I veered even further off the socially accepted path—into a world many neither understood nor believed in—the support I had once felt began to disappear. And with it, what felt like love came into question.

The questions from others were fast and relentless:

- Why would you leave a good career and a promising future?
- Why walk away from meaningful, socially responsible work?
- Why would you risk financial insecurity and personal rejection?

Why, Linda? Why?

The only answer I could give was: Because I had to.

I was both compelled and propelled. My soul knew that to not step forward would be to abandon my dream, my sacred purpose, and my promise to the Mother. I didn't know what lay beyond the curtain, but I knew something magnificent was waiting for me. I could feel it—calling me, beckoning me home.

And yet, for someone like me—someone who deeply yearns for love and connection—that decision tore me apart. The security blanket I thought I had been wrapped in was, in truth, woven from other people's expectations, fears, and definitions of love. I even asked a few trusted friends to keep an eye on the nearest mental health facility in case I disappeared. That's how intense the inner conflict was.

But here's what I discovered: That very unraveling was my invitation into Sacred Union with myself.

It compelled me to go deeper than I ever had before—to find within me a level of Sacred Love and inner union I didn't even know was possible. And that relationship, that inner harmony, is still evolving. It is not a one-time event. It is a river of grace—sometimes fast and wild, other times still and luminous. It flows within and around us, and it invites us, again and again, to sit beside it, to wade in, to dive deep, and to let it carry us Home.

Sacred Union is not something you chase. It is something you become. And it is glorious.

The Mother's Question

"Beloved angel, child of Our heart, what is the dream of Sacred Union that rests deep within thee? Far too often dearheart you judge yourself harshly rather than acknowledging the majesty of who you are—a child of One. You limit your sacred self in terms of Sacred Unions because you accommodate to what you believe you are deserving of rather than what you are truly capable of creating—and enjoying!

"My question to you is threefold and I guide you to set ego aside: What do you believe you are worthy of in terms of Sacred Union both within and without?

"And what do you desire from the deepest core of your being in terms of Union within and without?

"And what do you KNOW to be true in terms of what I choose to assist you in creating? Limitation or Wholeness?

"Surrender yourself to the dream sweet angel—it is your response to what you and We have designed prior to this incarnation. Allow us to assist you in this manifestation of your beauty, Truth and Wonder.

"Declare to your Sacred Self: I am willing to be in Sacred Union with my own radiant self. I am willing to meet others in love. Let that willingness be your quiet covenant."

Chapter Eight

The Art of Heart Communication

As we make this monumental shift in human consciousness—this elevation to a higher vibratory frequency—our minds naturally search for the essentials. What are the non-negotiables? What is the one thing without which this shift simply cannot happen?

The Divine Mother has answered this question with unwavering clarity:

> "In this cosmic theatre of transformation all the factors that we have discussed are vital supporting actors and crew creating the environment where heart consciousness can take place. But make no mistake about it, dearheart, heart speaking, heart listening, heart living commands center stage."

This is the bedrock of Nova Earth. This is the foundation upon which we build a new world—one that is not only kinder, brighter, and more workable, but one that honors the essence of who we are as divine beings in form.

Communication is a primary key to being human. It is how we shape and express our reality, how we co-create with each other and with the unseen realms. And now, as we step into the next octave of evolution, we are called to embrace a higher form of communication—Heart Conscious Communication.

The Divine Mother has made it unmistakably clear that true transformation begins and ends with the power of our words.

> "Your greatest Power is the Word and the most destructive power in the Universe is the abuse of that power.
>
> "Power is the ability to create, and that power is Divine. It is the child, the gift, the energy for the resurrection and ascension of the human race to remember and relearn the genuine application of usage of this divinely bestowed gift."

This is not optional. This is the turning point. Without a radical shift in the way we communicate—both with ourselves and with the world—we will fundamentally fail to bring Nova Earth into being.

We have spent years—lifetimes—internalizing the

principles of Sacred Love and Divine Union. We have embraced the truth that unless we love ourselves as sacred, we cannot be in genuine Unity with others. But now, it is time to extend this understanding outward, to revolutionize how we speak, how we listen, and how we express our divine essence in every exchange.

The questions before us are not small. They demand our full presence:

- How do we communicate in a way that actively fosters unity consciousness?
- How do we speak and listen—not just to one another—but to all realms, across dimensions and throughout the Universe?
- How do we retrain our hearts and minds, shifting our very language to reflect this massive evolution?
- What are the first steps? What are the guideposts? How do we make this shift not just possible, but unstoppable?

And perhaps the most raw and piercing questions of all:

- Do we truly have to leave behind the old patterns of blame, shame, guilt, and manipulation?
Do we really have to stand open, vulnerable, and exposed before one another?

The answer is YES.

Yes, because we are no longer bound by fear.

Yes, because we are capable of something greater.

Yes, because it is time.

This is not about rules or coercion; it is about alignment.

Heart Communication is not just a new way of speaking—it is a new way of being. It is the language of our sacred selves, the frequency of our divine nature made manifest.

And as we step fully into this truth, we do not merely talk about Unity. We become it.

Language as Living Energy

Language is more than just words. Language has the power to excite, empower, and create entirely new paradigms of behavior and experience. Our choice of words, tone, vibratory frequency, intent, gestures, and body language carries the ability to build, uplift—or just as easily, to divide and dismantle. It builds bridges—or burns them. It is also more than human speech.

Language is far more than a structured system of communication. It is a living expression of thought, emotion, and culture, an ever-evolving bridge that allows individuals and communities to share ideas, connect, and expand together. But at its essence, language is not just words—it's tone, frequency, intent and presence woven into form. Whether spoken, written, or expressed through symbols and gestures, language shapes reality, fosters understanding, and manifests creation itself.

Yet, true language extends beyond human speech. It includes the language of light, the frequencies of energy, and the profound currents of divine communication where insights, feelings, and knowing transcend the limitations of words. This is how the Universe whispers to us, how the heart speaks beyond sound, and how the soul remembers its eternal truth.

The Universal Language of the Heart

Language is not merely the dialects and sounds of a particular country or culture—it is our most basic form of heart connection, and as such, it is universal. When I asked the Council of Love to share tangible examples of this, they gave me two deeply personal experiences that sparkle to this day.

The Language of Channeling

Years ago, I was guided to teach a class on how to channel. The longing I have consistently heard in thousands of readings is always the same: "I wish I could do that." While I have always known that every single one of us has the innate ability to speak with our unseen spirit guides, I had never imagined actually teaching a class on the subject.

Then came the nudge from Archangel Gabrielle—

with whom I share a close and loving relationship. The idea of teaching channeling was both exhilarating and, truthfully, a little daunting. Fear and survival instincts peeked out from under the covers! What if I taught this so well, so thoroughly, that I worked myself out of an income?

That was a moment of choice. I had to walk through the fear and step forward in trust.

Looking back, those classes have not only been a huge success, but they have also been joyful, expansive, and deeply fulfilling. I have had the privilege of witnessing people blossom, stepping fully into their ability to communicate with their guides, guardian angels, and the Company of Heaven. The commitment of each individual and the cohesion of the practice groups has been astounding, a living example of Unity and community.

And now, Gabrielle has reminded me of something even greater: Channeling, in its purest and clearest form, is heart communication. It is heart speaking and heart listening.

The pattern has already been established. The shift to a higher frequency of language and communication is already unfolding, well underway.

The Unspoken Language of Understanding

The second experience I was reminded of took place years ago when I was visiting my dear friend, Donna, who worked in the tourism industry in Mexico.

It was a miserable winter back home in Ontario, Canada. I needed sun, rest, and an attitude adjustment. Donna, who was fluent in Spanish, had an evening shift one night and wanted me to spend time with a lovely friend of hers, Anna.

Happily accepting, we went to dinner together—only to realize, as we sat down, that neither of us spoke the other's language!

For a moment, we looked at each other. And then, we laughed. Instead of making it an issue, we simply enjoyed each other's company.

And here's the miracle: it wasn't until later that night that I realized something extraordinary. Anna had spoken in Spanish, I had spoken in English, and yet, we had absolutely understood everything the other had said.

We laughed. We shared. We connected, without a common spoken language. Did I see this as some kind of miracle or divine intervention? No. I knew in my heart that it was a pure, genuine gift of heart communication.

That is the true power of heart listening and

speaking—it transcends words, dissolving barriers, and allowing us to experience connection beyond language itself.

And that is the gift—a gift available to all who are willing to listen not just with the mind, but with the heart.

Star Family Language

Heart communication is not simply about speaking kindly or expressing our emotions, it is a sacred technology, a universal way of being. It is how we share the truth of who we are, beyond words, beyond fear, beyond misunderstanding. It is the language of Unity.

For years I've worked with the Unified Forces of the Outer Galaxies (UFOG), a delegation of enlightened star beings who come in peace to assist in our ascension.

Their presence among us is not new. They have been guiding and supporting Earth for millennia. These wise and ancient ones have lived through the rise and fall of civilizations, through destructive intergalactic wars fueled by ego, control, and division. They have seen planets lost to hatred, and through pain and perseverance, they chose another way. They chose peace.

Their wisdom, technologies, and understanding of dimensional science are far beyond our current human grasp. Traveling through white and black holes is to them what running to the market is for us. When they approached the perimeter of Earth's atmosphere, their first act was not conquest or interference, it was stabilization. They helped balance the planet's axis to prevent cataclysmic shifts that would have resulted in another ice age or worse. Their help has always been quiet, consistent, and rooted in reverence for our sovereignty.

One of the most beautiful gifts they have shared is their language—or rather, the evolution of language they underwent after the intergalactic wars. They knew that if conflict was ever to truly end, communication itself had to evolve. The way beings spoke and listened had to reflect their intention for peace.

They developed four forms of communication, each with a distinct purpose. And through this evolution, they eventually arrived at a language that is a direct expression of the heart. This language is called Saedor, and it is the purest embodiment of heart communication.

Let's briefly explore the four forms to understand how Saedor came to be:

1. Perro (pair-o)

Perro is neutral, fact-based communication. It transmits information without emotional bias—simple, clear data that can be shared across cultures and species. After the wars, Perro was used to re-establish dialogue where trust had been broken. It helped different beings begin to speak again, without misunderstanding or emotional distortion.

2. Paca (pack-a)

Paca is the language of emotion. It conveys how someone feels but may or may not reflect truth or clarity. It is widely used on Earth, where we often mistake emotional expression for complete communication. While it reveals our inner state, it doesn't necessarily build bridges of understanding on its own.

3. Badu (baa-too)

Badu is persuasive language, a mix of emotion and information designed to prompt action. It can be motivating or manipulative. On Earth, Badu is dominant in politics, media, and marketing. It's often reactive and divisive, appealing to ego, fear, pride, or desire. It's used to push people into doing, rather than inviting them into being.

4. Saedor (say-door)

And then there is Saedor.

The crown jewel of this evolution, Saedor is heart-centered, balanced, and deeply sacred. It incorporates fact, emotion, and lived experience, but always in the spirit of mutual respect, unity, and understanding. In

Saedor, all communication is anchored in truth—not just personal truth, but Universal truth.

It is offered from the heart, received by the heart, and honors the divinity in both speaker and listener.

Saedor is not about winning an argument or convincing anyone of anything. It is about connection. It is about creating space where each being can be seen, heard, and felt in the fullness of who they are. This is what heart communication truly is.

At the core of Saedor is a principle known as Divine Neutrality. It is the foundation of all genuine heart speaking and heart listening.

Divine Neutrality

Divine Neutrality is not indifference or detachment. It is the luminous center between extremes. It is a state of being where we hold all perspectives in compassion, without losing our anchor in Love.

It does not mean we feel nothing—it means we do not get swept away by judgment or ego. We stay rooted in the knowing that all experiences, all voices, all stories have a place in the great unfolding. From this place, we speak with clarity, we listen with openness, and we respond with wisdom.

Divine Neutrality allows us to be present in the storm

without becoming the storm. It allows us to disagree without separation. It invites us to live, speak, and listen from the sacred center of the heart, where peace exists.

This is the kind of communication the Earth is asking for now. This is the frequency that brings healing.

…This is the way of Saedor.

And now, beloveds, allow me to step aside so you may receive directly from one of our dearest allies and friends in the stars: Galea, Communications Officer of the Unified Forces of the Outer Galaxies. She has often been a bridge between our hearts and theirs, bringing wisdom, light, and laughter in equal measure.

A Message from Galea, Communications Officer, UFOG

"Do we come in peace to assist in this beautiful reconstruction of Gaia, this place of such phenomenal beauty and tenderness, this Archangel in form?

"We do come in peace, and we come bearing gifts!

"Are there many things that we give and have already planted in your societies that assist in this expansion of heart and soul? Yes.

"We cannot come as the 'rescuers' because what that does is diminish—and disregard—your Divine

Authority, your sovereignty, your free will.

"We know you understand this. But, sweet ones, the time is close! The number of sightings is undeniable, and as you shift collectively into this ability to embrace—not out of fear—then we make our presence clearly known... and yes, bring more presents!

"I wished to simply be able to give you a little update and to remind you of Saedor—and to practice it—because this is your new language in the Mother's New Time."

Practicing Saedor: A Heart Communication Activation

Let us now turn inward and begin to feel this sacred language—not as something to learn with the mind, but to remember with the heart.

You may read this as a meditation, speak it aloud, or simply allow yourself to receive it as a transmission.

Begin by taking a deep breath. Place your hand on your heart. Feel the steady rhythm of your own sacred life force.

I am safe to speak from my heart.

I am safe to be still and to listen.

I am safe to be seen.

I am safe to see others in their wholeness.

I open now to Divine Neutrality…

I release all judgment.

I let go of needing to be right or needing to be understood.

Instead, I choose Love.

I choose clarity.

I choose freedom.

May my words be offerings of peace.

May my listening be a sanctuary.

May my voice carry the frequency of my soul.

I remember the language of the stars.

I remember the language of my own heart.

I speak now, and always, in Saedor, the language of Love.

Breathe that in. Feel the gentleness, the neutrality, the warmth.

And as you go about your day, know that each word you speak from your heart is part of the symphony of New Earth.

Speaking from the Waves of Love

When you feel ready—when your heart is steady and your body is calm—I invite you to speak the following affirmation aloud.

Let your voice be your breath made sacred. Let your breath be your Love in motion.

Visualize your sound waves moving across the Earth, infusing the air, the soil, the waters, and every heart with the harmony of Love and Unity. Let it ripple outward, not just across the planet, but into the farthest reaches of the universe.

For many years, the Divine Mother has shown us the image of waves within her infinite ocean of being—a gentle yet profound way to help us understand how energy flows and travels.

All of existence is in motion. Everything is vibrating, singing its own song, dancing in waves of frequency and light. This is especially true of spoken language.

Our words are not simply air and sound—they are vibrations that move through the unified field, intersecting with brainwaves, electromagnetic currents, and the very frequencies that shape our consciousness. Sound waves influence brain waves. Cosmic waves alter planetary grids. We are constantly swimming in this radiant ocean of energy, brushing up against each other's frequencies, whether we are aware of it or not.

And now, right now, many of you are beginning to hear in new ways. Some of you are experiencing the activation of what has long been dormant: an inner hearing, a sacred resonance. You may begin to notice the hum of the universe, the music of the spheres, the whispers of Source. This is part of your spiritual evolution. This is your divine design awakening.

With the support of our star family, the guidance of the Divine Mother, and your own sovereign will, you are expanding. Your consciousness is tuning into new wavelengths of perception—higher, broader, deeper than ever before. You are being attuned to perceive what was once invisible. To sense what once lay beyond reach. To remember what you have always known, that you are love.

And as this capacity deepens, as your heart becomes more finely tuned, your choices begin to shift. You find yourself drawn toward more mature, more truthful, more loving ways of communicating.

This is the gift of heart speaking.

This is the sacred blessing of heart listening.

So, once again, take a breath. Place your hand over your heart.

And if you are ready, speak this aloud—not only for yourself, but for all beings across all realms and timelines:

I choose to speak from my heart.

I choose to listen with Love.

I choose the frequency of Unity.

I send my voice across the waves of creation—

As a beacon of peace,

A call to harmony,

And a song of remembering.

I remember and claim who I AM.

I remember and claim who we are.

I speak now, and always, in Saedor

Let your voice echo as light. Let your breath become a wave of love that travels endlessly.

You are part of the Great Symphony now.

And your heart, dear one, is the instrument of the New Earth.

Shifting to Heart Communication

Now you have felt what the energy of Speaking in Saedor is, the question is how do you translate this higher frequency knowing into the practical application of your everyday form of communication—both within and without.

One of the challenges of communication today is that there is a tendency to be reactive and even strident. This has been exacerbated by the prevalence of social media engagement, text technology, and news programming that is on-inclusive. All too often there is an internal and external expectation to react or respond without considering the context, motivation, tone or underlying motivation or even need. Communication has become a constant background chatter that fills up our heads but not our hearts.

So, what are the practical steps that we can utilize to shift our communication both personally and publicly the higher frequency of heart centered speaking and listening?

One of the stumbling blocks that may create hesitancy in shifting to this frequency of communication is that folks think that in order to do so, they have to have done their work. While knowing more about your soul design, your sacred purpose, your guardian angels, your core issues is always expansive and helpful in genuinely engaging in heart communication, it is not a necessity.

In many ways, opening to the desire for a clearer more expansive inclusive form of authentic conversation can simply reveal and even at times address those processes. It is part of the unseen energetic gifts and downloads that we have been receiving from our unseen friends and from the Mother/Father/One. In fact, as your heart opens that cosmic soul information simply begins to flow. While we are discussing the how to's and practicalities of inter-personal communication, understand you are also addressing your conversations with the human collective and our unseen friends in the rafters. They are mutually inclusive.

The practice of genuine communication by its very nature includes both heart speaking, heart listening and heart hearing. It is balanced because a genuine exchange can only occur when all those features are present. It is important also to understand that heart speaking and particularly heart listening and hearing are not always verbal, an out loud response.

The starting point of shifting to heart speaking and heart listening, heart-hearing is being deeply aware of your internal dialogue. Those internal conversations with your beautiful sacred self, between your head and heart or your ego, mental, emotional, physical and soul self are fundamental to understanding how your social patterns have been formulated and grounded. Our internal dialogue, formulated and anchored since birth, determines our attitudes, expressions and patterns of communication, and certainly our conversational styles.

As we delve into our how to's of heart communication, the steps, the holding of Divine Neutrality, be aware that the starting point of each of these shifts in consciousness commences with a deep honest meaningful conversation with your sacred self.

Returning to Divine Neutrality

Earlier in this chapter, I touched upon Divine Neutrality as an integral part of heart communication. Before we go further into the practical how-to's, I invite you to pause and come into deeper alignment with this essential quality.

Why? Because in my experience and observation, Divine Neutrality is perhaps the most challenging—and most transformative—aspect of heart communication. It is the foundation upon which we shift into the higher frequency of what it means to be a Nova Gaian: not only committed to, but actively participating in the co-creation of a new world that works for everyone.

Divine Neutrality is a state of being. It is where we embody divine balance and sacred impartiality—symbolically holding the energy of neutrality without needing to be above or below, monarch or servant.

It is not passive. It is presence—an anchored place from which we are not swayed by extremes, but remain steady in love, wisdom, and refined discernment. Free from judgment, free from ego, free from attachment to outcomes.

Divine Neutrality allows us to listen deeply, to speak clearly, and to hold space for all perspectives—without condemnation or superiority—recognizing and embracing the divinity within all beings. Divine

Neutrality is a key component of how to practice the art of heart communication.

The How To's of Heart Communication

The very real shift to Heart Communication is not about adding one more task or technique to your spiritual to-do list. It is about the surrender—surrendering the need to be right and surrendering the right to judge.

Understand: there is a world of difference between agreement about fact or position, and respect for others.

Far too often in our human interactions, validation is awarded to those who are seen as factually or perceptively "correct." In this race for the winner's circle, we alienate ourselves—not only from the sacred truth of our own hearts, but from each other. Far too often we see that the most strident loudest voice is assumed to be correct rather than the most sensitive balanced approach.

In the friction of wanting to be acknowledged, we engage in self-defeating behavior. We react instead of respond. And auto-response is neither honoring nor truly engaging – it seeks to eliminate the give and take exchange of a genuine conversation.

The primary rule of heart communication is simple: Stop the need to immediately respond to everything that crosses your screen or ears.

The key to heart communication lies in the pause—in

taking that sacred moment to truly listen.

What is really being said?

What is the question or statement truly about?

What is the subtext?

What is the motivation behind the words?

When we auto-respond, we do so from programming—much like Pavlov's dog.

But what most people are seeking, even within the most defensive or provocative words, is "Am I heard?"

Because we've been taught that being heard means we have value. Think of how often in your life you've heard the words "Do you hear me?" Or "I hear you."

These are not just phrases—they are pleas for affirmation. They are soul-level signposts.

Heart listening and heart responding do not require speed, nor do they require agreement. You are not reacting—you are receiving. You are listening from your heart of love, not from the ego-mind or the emotional battlefield.

This kind of listening allows you to perceive what's beneath the words. You respond not from judgment, but from your heart knowing, from reverence—for the other and for your own sacred self.

There is no requirement for agreement—only the soul

agreement that you will not judge. Heart communication is being in active engagement, a subtle promise that you will hear, discern, and respond from your heart.

Whether you are the initiator or responder, heart speaking is about creating sacred space—space for honest, kind, respectful exchange.

The value of simple casual conversation is often underrated and not understood as an incredibly powerful tool of building bridges and connections. Casual conversation, when infused with presence, can become a profound act of Love. You are saying to the other person "You are worth my time. You are worth my energy." And in a world where so many have forgotten their value, this is soul-affirming beyond measure.

Heart speaking is not hasty. It is thoughtful, considerate, and strong—but never strident. It includes the moment to ask the Divine Mother's simple and eternal question: "Is it of Love?"

It gives yourself the grace to pause. It gives the other the dignity of receiving a real response. Whether you take a breath or a day, you create space for meaningful exchange to take place.

Practicing Heart Speaking & Heart Listening

As the channel for the Council of Love I teach and facilitate a wide variety of classes on various topics.

Every class, every meeting is infused with the respect and tenderness of heart speaking and listening.

In discussing this shift in our human communication paradigm attendees will often express a yearning for that shift but also a disbelief in the ability of the collective to truly emerge to a higher, kinder, more engaging form of communication exchange. The belief in their innate power to alter the human paradigm is not present. And yet the Council repeatedly tells us that the change must come from the grassroots. It is the only way in which the shift is sustainable and empowering.

In these conversations when I bring mention the examples of channeled messages and our star family, the refrain is often that, "they are not human—they live on a higher dimensional plain—the are in a different frequency and they do not need to deal with the density of the current aggressive and arrogant forms of communication we seem surrounded by."

But we do have human examples all around us—some notable and some as close as your next-door neighbor. Consider the communication role models such as Jesus or Lao Tzu, the Dalai Lama or Michael Beckwith. Consider the powerful words of truth from Nelson Mandela: "No one is born hating another person because of the color of his skin, or his background, or his religion. People must learn to hate, and if they can learn to hate, they can be taught to love, for love comes more naturally to the human heart than its opposite," and "Love everyone, including yourself. Humanity is my race and love knows no boundaries."

There are living thriving examples of heart communication all around us if we stop for a moment to observe. They are not the glaring voices demanding attention. They are the engaged speakers and listeners who are willing to have a respectful expansive exchange. They do not feel threatened in speaking what they believe to be fair and just. They are willing to hear the other person's thoughts—not being spoken over but in a genuine heart exchange.

Those folks are clearly present all around us. Recently, I came across this article written by the owner of a British pub in a nearby town. The owner had recently expanded his business by opening a second pub and apparently had some negative reaction from patrons. He wrote:

"We have learnt a lot after our move four weeks ago. One thing that is plainly clear, is karaoke doesn't work for us on a weeknight when people are joining us to eat and have a social drink, and our service and ambiance suffer because of it. Last night, we had issues which we can only apologize for, we had a few complaints which we hold our hands up to. So, there will no longer be karaoke on Thursdays, you will still be able to enjoy it late night from 10 p.m. on a Sunday if that's your thing. Thank you."

This is a down-to-earth example of heart speaking and heart listening. There was a problem, the owner not only listened, but he also heard. He didn't jump to defensive behavior but reached out, took corrective action and offered his apology for misreading his clientèle. A win-win in the most ordinary of circumstances. I would go to this pub because I feel that they care about how they engage with folks. And as Nova Gaians, so do we!

Take the time, make the effort to not only find those current human examples in your life but to be one. Engage in caring nurturing kind conversations—the will feed your soul. Heart speaking and heart listening is not about acquiescence; it is about empowerment. It is so desirable, so needed that this will spread like wildfire, but warm your heart like a cozy campfire.

As this practice continues, it becomes viral—because love is viral.

The desire to be seen and heard is embedded in our human DNA. It is soul reaching out to soul, heart conjoining with heart.

Do not expect overnight perfection.

This is a path of practice, patience, and courage — especially as we rewire our responses in a reactive world.

But take heart, sweet angels: This shift happens far more quickly than you might imagine.

And when it does, you will begin to feel it—in the joy,

in the texture,

in the tone,

and in the true substance of your conversations.

The Mother's Question

The questions posed by the Divine Mother guiding our shift in perspective and gently leading us to a deeper embrace of the truth of who we really are. The Mother's Question reminds us that to expand into genuine heart communication, there must be surrender of what does not serve:

"Beloved Child, what have you and are you willingly surrendering? What no longer serves you either within your sacred field and/or without. Because sweet angel you know that both are mirrors of each other. In your Divine Neutrality, with the full presence of your Divine Knowing, what do you willingly set aside as it is no longer of service to you or the collective? Bless what you surrender in the name of Love and do not look back, for you are making room for the new."

"What is the new element (the Never Ending Wonderful element) that you are embracing to fill the space left by what you are and have surrendered? Will you now surrender to Our sweet embrace and fully partake of the feast that We have prepared for you?"

Take time to truly ponder and receive this kind and nurturing message from the Mother – do not hurry! It is truly worthwhile to make notes of what comes up for you as you ponder and process what you are surrendering—what no longer serves you or those you love. Your reflection will not only render a deeper understanding of your sacred self, it will inform you not only of what you choose to surrender but what you yearn to make room for, the aspects of your sacred self and this life you are creating.

Consider how you really wish to communicate with yourself and others. How do you wish to be spoken to, communicated with? What is the texture and tenor, the sub-text and flavor that you yearn to bring to engagement in future conversations?

Remember the Mother has told us that the Word is our strongest power.

This is a question you may return to again, and again. It is richly rewarding when you come back at a later point in this journey of Spiritual Rebellion—the choosing of Unity, to see just how far you have traveled-what this shift has not only entailed but meant to you and others. Journal, note, remember dearheart.

Chapter Nine

The Framework of Unity Consciousness

There is an architecture of light, unseen yet eternal, rising within us and around us — the blueprint of a new world, written in the Language of Love.

In recent years, an extraordinary expansion has been quietly blossoming across the planet — so natural, so organic, that many have barely noticed. And yet, it has changed everything. This is the nature of true spiritual evolution: gradual, unseen, until it is everywhere, undeniable. Subtle.

So, it is with the Divine Architecture of Nova Earth. The framework of Unity is already here, woven into the very fabric of existence. It is not theory or metaphor, but living design—an energetic scaffolding, a sacred infrastructure strong enough to hold the dawning age of Love. These are not simply beautiful concepts; they are universal constants, living states of being, the eternal principles that allow Unity Consciousness to not only arise but to thrive.

These we call the Pillars of Unity. They are woven together, like luminous beams of light, creating a foundation sturdy enough to hold a world of peace, love, and true creation. These Pillars include:

- Sacred Love—the animating force of all life, the core vibration of the Cosmos, and the birthplace of all creation.
- Divine Authority—the sacred sovereignty within us, the right and responsibility to co-create with Source, in perfect alignment with Universal Law and Love.
- Harmonizing & Divine Radiance—the ever-present flow of Divine Light and Energy that uplifts, unifies, and infuses all beings.
- Divine Knowing—the heart-and-soul intelligence that transcends logic; the innate truth we recognize through resonance, not reason.
- Divine Neutrality—the sacred ability to remain in compassionate observation, beyond judgment or polarity, rooted in the stillpoint of Source.

These are not lofty ideas. They are the non-negotiables, the load-bearing beams of Nova Gaia herself. They are the constants that allow the structure of Nova Gaia to stand firm through all the winds of change. They are what we return to when we wobble, and what we lean upon as we build the NEW.

Because we are speaking of Divine Architecture, we

will be weaving deeply with the channeled guidance from the Council of Love—the architects, the master builders, and the keepers of this sacred design.

I invite you to journey deeply now—to feel in your very bones—how Divine Authority naturally unfolds into Divine Knowing, how Divine Knowing blossoms into Divine Neutrality, and how from that sacred ground, the great flowering of Unity emerges.

Divine Authority

From the very beginning, we have been entrusted with Divine Authority—the power and responsibility of free will. This is not the authority of domination, hierarchy, or control. It is the sacred alignment of our choices with Love and the Divine Plan.

And yet, one of the conundrums of human existence is our insatiable drive to be in control of our life, choices, decisions, while simultaneously yearning to be taken care of. Admittedly, recognized or not, there is that vulnerable part of us that yearns to be seen, heard, attended to and taken care of—while still maintaining our sovereignty.

The Divine in birthing humanity has imbued each of us with free will—it is the foundation of our existence upon the planet. The Divine Mother tells us that free will is her compliment and act of faith in our ability to transcend the old paradigms and create the NEW. It is the supreme act of confidence and trust in our ability to create lives and environments which are in alignment with our individual and collective divine designs as well as the Universal Laws of Love.

When free will is negated, interfered with or denied, those are human actions born of human volition. The Divine did not create a race of slaves, quite the contrary—we are the Divine Mother's Activators. Free will, our divine sovereignty, is our foremost divine inheritance. It is the foundational tenet of existence here upon Gaia.

However, there has often been a human tendency to question that birthright of free will. That question is born of adhering to old patterns of humanity that have denied this basic tenant. Because of that, the COL, the Divine Mother and company of heaven repeatedly remind and reassured us of our free will sovereignty.

There are continually strong reminders regarding our Divine Authority—about claiming it, using it, honoring it and wisely choosing how we create our reality. Archangel Michal tells us:

"Your existence starts with Divine Authority. You cannot surrender Divine Authority—it's your sovereign birthright—it is your divine Inheritance…"

The Divine Mother explains:

"Divine authority means choosing with your free will and your Divine Authority of free will, to direct how, where, when, if you choose to proceed.

"You have the most magnificent internal wisdom and knowing. It is an illusion for you to even conceive or believe or think that you are not in your Divine Authority every moment of your existence. If you choose to ignore it then you are not fulfilling your joy, your purpose or what gives you the greatest glee.

Yes, there are moments when those decisions can be challenging and difficult. But that shows you your strength, your courage, your valor, your persistence in working your way back to us."

Divine Authority: A Loving Invitation from the Mother

Dearhearts, you were born not just with love, but as Love—as living sparks of the Divine, carrying the pattern of All That Is. From the beginning, the Mother designed this journey with purpose: not to test or punish, but to guide each of us back into the fullness of our being. Into our Creator selves. Into Divine Authority.

This isn't the authority of domination or control, but the sacred power of alignment—with Love, with Divine Will, with your own infinite heart. It is the authority to choose, to lead, to create, to steward your life and this world with conscious intention. It is the divine permission to step into the truth of who you are.

The Mother reminds us: You are not here to be puppets or bystanders. You are here as co-creators. You are entrusted with the watercolors of existence, the building blocks of Nova Earth, not to be micromanaged, but to be empowered.

With that comes the invitation to assume the Divine Authority that is already yours—not someday, but now.

Yes, humanity has known the shadow side of authority—the misuse, the pain, the patterns of abandonment and betrayal. But those were chapters, not conclusions. Now we step into a new story.

To assume Divine Authority is to lovingly take the reins of your own life—your thoughts, your choices, your environment, your actions—in alignment with Love and purpose. It means no longer drifting, but steering. No longer fearing but trusting.

It doesn't mean you walk alone. Quite the opposite. The Mother, the archangels, and your star family walk with you, breathe with you, and lift you every step of the way. Your energy is not finite—not when it is plugged into the infinite Source of Love. When your actions arise from joy and service, you are never depleted, only renewed.

And yes, we are meant to walk this path together. Not as hierarchical structures, but as circles of collaboration—where each voice, each gift, each vision is essential. This is not top-down command; it is soul-to-soul co-creation.

So, if you ask, "Am I ready?"

Know this: You were made for this time.

Let your heart lead. Let your Love guide your actions. And if a choice or path doesn't feel like Love, pause, breathe, ask, and realign.

You have the divine right, the divine responsibility, to create from Love. To lead from peace. To shape this world into one of laughter, kindness, truth, and Unity. That is Divine Authority.

And the Mother is here. Always. Whispering in your ear:

"You are ready. You are worthy. And you are never alone."

Harmonizing with Divine Radiance

In 2023, a monumental gift from the Mother began to flood the planet: Divine Radiance—the living breath of the One. This Radiance, infused directly from the Heart of the Mother, began to awaken every molecule of Gaia and every cell of our being.

Receiving Divine Radiance is as natural as breathing. It is not something we must earn or strive for—it is the expanded field in which we now live and move.

> "You have received a gift, and it is the beginning of the gifts. Open your sweet hearts even wider, sweet ones. Allow yourself to receive." – The Mother

Divine Radiance activates transformation, transmutation, elimination, and elevation within us. It gently but powerfully harmonizes our inner landscape, naturally releasing what no longer belongs and magnifying the essence of our soul design. It is the pure substance of creation—flowing, expanding, refining, uplifting.

Harmonizing and Sacred Union are pivotal aspects of the ascension process. At its core, ascension is a journey of transformation to a higher vibrational state of being. It's an expansion of our consciousness, transcending the limits of the physical world to embrace a higher, more profound understanding of reality.

The Divine Mother reminds us:

> "Divine Radiance does not simply beam and bounce off—it infuses every aspect, core and expression of your being. You live, exist, within an unlimited ever-expanding universe and therefore sweet angels you, in alignment with My Plan and your infinite and eternal design, are unlimited and ever expanding."

At the heart of this transformation is Sacred Union: the internal merging of the Divine Feminine and Divine Masculine within each of us. These are not genders, but archetypal energies—intuition and compassion blending with action and strength. Sacred Union is the anchoring of wisdom, where wholeness becomes the platform for our expansion.

And from that Sacred Union arises Harmonizing, not as a passive state, but as a living, breathing dance with All That Is.

> "In this shift that I have activated and which is well underway, there is a leaving-behind of the old… It is the harmonization of all elements, and you within this environment of all elements."—The Divine Mother

Harmonizing is the alignment of our thoughts, emotions, actions, and spiritual practices with the highest frequencies of Love, compassion, and Divine Knowing. It is choosing to breathe and live as the true Nova Gaians we are.

Personal Reflection: Harmonizing with Divine Radiance

My first true experience of harmonizing with Divine Radiance transformed not only my perspective—it transformed my life.

It was a simple evening, sitting in my favorite spot, watching the sunset. The sky was ablaze with color, the breeze soft against my skin. I am accustomed to feeling the beauty of such moments, letting peace and gratitude fill my heart. But on this day, as I consciously accepted the Mother's invitation to harmonize with Divine Radiance, everything changed.

The Mother had guided me: "This is not something to be studied, but to be experienced." And so, I sat, heart and arms wide open, welcoming.

But as I sat there something so unexpected, so precious and wonderful occurred. I was transported. I was no longer just admiring the sky, the clouds, the trees, the air—I was one with them. I was the sky, the clouds, the air. In this harmony there was no separation—I knew and felt them—all of them, their essence, their energy, their dreams, their knowing—all flowed through me, as me. There was no separation, no observer. Only Unity. Only Love. Only Being.

In those sacred hours, a truth was anchored in my heart forever: we are not separate—not from Gaia, the elements nor from each other. We are one living, breathing, radiant Unified Field of One.

This experience, this merging with Divine Radiance, is not reserved for a few. It is the birthright of all. Do it, invite this experience into your being!

Living Harmonization: The Mother's Invitation

"How do you do this?" The Mother asks. "By harmonizing with yourself, within our arms, within our embrace, within my heart."

Harmonizing is an experiential path. It cannot be fully known through thought alone. It is an expansion—breathing, living, playing—in alignment with the sacredness of All.

It is not about achieving perfect balance as humans might measure it. It is about blending, matching, merging—like the perfect ingredients of a divine recipe, creating a whole that is greater than the sum of its parts.

When we harmonize, we are not losing our individuality, our Divine Authority, or our sacred purpose. Rather, we are becoming more of who we are—living creators in Unity.

The Mother explains:

"You are inviting everybody in—to the dinner, to the picnic, to the mountain, to the sea—and saying: Come join me. Come feel the fragrance of expansion. There is no hurry. There is no desperation. It is not either/or; it is ALL. Let us harmonize!"

We extend our arms and invite the world—people, animals, nature, situations—into our field. Not to control them, but to allow them to experience the harmony of merging, of being within and through us. And in this sacred inclusion, everything begins to shift.

The Mother is very clear: the term Embracing must be

part of our understanding. To harmonize is to embrace. To breathe in all that seeks healing, Unity, and Love. It is a level of merger and conjoining which allows each of us to find a new rhythm in our shared heart.

This is the true expansion of Divine Radiance: embracing and harmonizing, inside and out, across the entire field of our lives.

And as we breathe… we expand… we allow the alchemy of Divine Radiance to do its perfect work.

This pillar of Harmonizing with Divine Radiance is an essential element upon which we build Nova Gaia and anchor Unity Consciousness. Leaning into this gift is not about starting over. It is about embracing our role, our responsibility, our joy at being pioneers of the NEW, beloved Angels of Light.

"I invite you to experience this with me," the Mother says.
"Breathe, ground, observe the subtleties, because you are the lens of perception of the collective. You are the ones that say, 'Something's different.' And indeed it is."

Harmonizing with Divine Radiance is not a future event. It is here. It is now. It is the pathway home — to yourself, to Gaia, to One. Let us walk it together, hand in hand, heart to heart to heart.

The Mother's Question:

"Sweet angels of my heart, are you willing to embrace yourself, your world, and All within my arms of Divine Radiance, and to breathe the harmony of Love into every breath, every step, every dream? Do you choose to accept, to claim as your divine inheritance of knowing you are within the Unified Field of One?"

Take the time and allow yourself to embrace and to be embraced by the sweetness of being in Unity—of knowing that you are an integral part of One, of All.

Divine Knowing

At the heart of the framework is Divine Knowing—the deep, soul-rooted recognition of truth by resonance. It is the quiet clarity that stirs in our hearts when something is aligned, and the subtle abrasion we feel when something is not.

This Knowing does not require proof or argument. It is a grace given at birth, though often forgotten under the noise of doubt and conditioning.

It is one of the Pillars in the sacred architecture of Nova Earth, and a fundamental quality of your own sacred self. It is the part of you that has always been connected to the Divine—not only accessing Divine Wisdom but participating in it. Ever evolving, ever eternal.

There is a part of us, far too often denied or dismissed, that I call heart knowing.

It's when we simply know beyond question what is. It may be about a person, a situation, an outcome—it is like our soul's own Google, offering the answer in an instant. We cannot always explain it. It may even be challenged by the outside world. But within the discernment of our heart and soul, the knowing stands unwavering, omnipresent.

We know what love feels like.

We know the fragrance of truth.

We recognize it not by logic, but by the resonance that stirs deep within our being.

As Archangel Gabrielle so beautifully shares, Divine Knowing is the deep-rooted sense of alignment with the Divine Perfection within ourselves and within all beings. It is a state where there is no doubt, no wavering—only a profound harmony with Source that guides us, both in this life and beyond.

Yet the key, always, is Trust. Trust in the tender whisper of your own heart. Trust in the radiant thread of Love that moves through all things. Trust that when you stand in your Divine Knowing, you are already exactly where you need to be.

The Divine Mother, in Her infinite wisdom, expands our understanding of this trust.

For eons, humanity has come to know Love through outward experience—through expressions, relationships, fleeting moments of grace. But now, She beckons us deeper: into the full embodiment of Love within ourselves.

When we encounter that which is not of Love, it feels abrasive, discordant, like sandpaper on the soul. This discomfort is not punishment—it is guidance. It is the clarity of Divine Knowing rising within us, showing us what aligns and what does not.

We do not need to judge.

We do not need to attack or defend.

Instead, we stand in our heart, our mind, our will—anchored in Divine Neutrality—and we proceed with the wisdom of Love.

Thus, Divine Knowing becomes not just an act of remembrance, but a way of being, a sacred stance from which we co-create the New Earth.

And into this sacred unfolding steps Archangel Uriel, Keeper of Divine Authority and Divine Knowing.

Uriel reminds us that this journey of Divine Knowing is not a burden or a task—it is Sacred Play. He invites us to breathe in his shimmering silver essence, to envision ourselves seated upon our Silver Throne—the throne of Divine Authority and Divine Knowing—where our alignment with truth becomes natural and effortless.

He gently reminds us:

"Divine Knowing is not something newly given; it is something ancient within us. It has simply fallen into disuse for many, hidden beneath layers of societal conditioning, disbelief, and the longing for acceptance. But now, it is reawakened. It is reactivated. And through simple, joyful practice, the matrix of Divine Knowing will be restored to its natural brilliance."

Uriel encourages us to begin simply, lightly, playfully—to relax into the practice.

To breathe in his Silver Flame of Illumination, to let clarity flood our being, and to allow Divine Knowing to arise effortlessly from within.

And then, as we sit more firmly upon the throne of our own knowing, comes the sacred reminder from Lord Melchizedek—the wisdom keeper of Divine Order and Alignment.

Melchizedek speaks with the clarity of one who sees our essence fully:

He reminds us that our Divine Knowing is inseparable from our Divine Authority.

That our authority—our right to speak, to act, to create in alignment with Love — is not something granted by the world, but by the very fact of our existence.

"Your divine authority comes from your divine right to exist.

And in the assumption of your right and your authority—not as a title or a mantle to be worn, but as the anchoring of truth within your heart—you align with Source, with One, with Mother/Father/God. You align with Love itself."

Melchizedek gently reminds us that in choosing to trust our Divine Knowing, we also choose to trust who we are: the amazing, anchored, present, physical angel-hybrids that we are, here and now.

This is not arrogance. It is not ambition. It is the pure, sacred acknowledgment of our being.

Thus, Divine Knowing is not only about sensing the truth.

It is about living it.

Speaking it.

Acting from it.

Being it.

It is the simple, radiant certainty that the Light within us is real, is trusted, and is already aligned with the Heart of One.

Sweet angels, we KNOW the world has struggled and stumbled, that for far too long, ego, arrogance, abuse, and violence have cast long shadows.

We KNOW—with the quiet certainty of our hearts—that this must change for a world of peace, kindness, and Unity to truly blossom. There have been moments when we felt unsure, questioning where to turn or how to begin. But always, within us, the light of Divine Knowing has remained steady. Now, the gift before us is gentle and profound: to trust what we know, and to tenderly, courageously weave that Divine Knowing into every choice, every creation, every new beginning. We are ready. And we are not alone.

With every breath, with every step, let your Divine Knowing be the love that lights the way—for you are the living promise of a new Earth.

Divine Neutrality

The final piece of the spiritual architecture of Unity Consciousness is perhaps the most courageous: Divine Neutrality.

Divine Neutrality is not indifference. It is not passivity. It is not uniformity.

It is the active, vibrant anchoring in the heart of love where judgment cannot survive.

It is the capacity to hold sacred space for all beings, all

paths, all perspectives—without rushing to categorize, correct, or conquer. It is the place beyond "right" and "wrong," where the only measure is whether we are acting from Love, Wisdom, and the highest vision of Unity.

A Misunderstood Teaching

There are differing beliefs about what Divine Neutrality actually means. Some view Source as indifferent—a cosmic non-interventionist. Others believe in a system of divine judgment, where God rewards or punishes according to merit.

But the Council's teaching on Divine Neutrality transcends these extremes. It is not detachment or indifference, and it is not judgment disguised as righteousness.

Rather, Divine Neutrality is the ability to enter—and stay within—a judgment-free zone. It is constancy. It is sacred space. It is the quiet confidence of Divine Knowing—the inner recognition of truth, even when truth is not being shouted.

Anchoring Divine Neutrality

When you anchor in Divine Neutrality, it holds you. It becomes the field from which Sacred Love and Divine Union flow through your words, gestures, and presence.

It allows you to respect others' beliefs, paths, and

expressions—even when they diverge from your own. It is not about agreement. It is about willingness—the willingness to listen, to allow, to witness, and to respond without needing to control or convert.

In the current climate of controversy and reactive noise, this can feel challenging. But it is also one of the most powerful ways we lead—silently, steadily—as Divine Influencers and Divine Activators.

Divine Neutrality does not override your inner knowing. It holds space with your Divine Knowing. You still discern what is true, what is incomplete, what is manipulation or misalignment—but you do so without judgment. You recognize that holding a polarity of right/wrong, correct/incorrect, blocks true heart communication.

When you listen from the heart—without the compulsion to be right or to fix—you begin to hear what is really being said. Including the spaces between the words. The sacred subtext.

Why is Divine Neutrality so challenging?

Humanity has been steeped in the tribal need to be "right," to secure identity, belonging, and power. Our opinions became our shields. Our positions became our homes.

But in the process, we have fractured the very

community, trust, and Unity we so deeply crave. This false architecture of separation has reached critical mass—leading to division, loneliness, violence, and societal breakdown.

We often tend to cherish our beliefs and opinions because it often provides a sense of empowerment, even superiority. Our beliefs and opinions about ourselves and the world, even the Universe, allow us to feel like we are "on track" in a world that is often confusing, confrontational and alienating. Hence, the challenge to adopt, hold and maintain a position of neutrality becomes personally ever more challenging, strenuous and laborious.

The solution cannot come from choosing new sides. The solution is to step outside of sides altogether. It is to be the space where all beings are honored, even when we passionately disagree.

The Good News: Nova Earth's Blueprint Already Exists

We are not creating Divine Neutrality from scratch. The Framework of Unity Consciousness — the divine grid of love, balance, and wisdom—is already fully present upon Gaia. That grid and pathway already shine with luminous clarity. It is vibrant. It is alive. It is simply waiting for our heart declaration of Yes!

Each time you choose neutrality, true neutrality,

you are not struggling alone. You are accessing and amplifying the living grid of Nova Earth.

How do we Embody Divine Neutrality?

How do we translate that to our behaviors as co-creators of Nova Earth? As Divine Activators and Influencers?

Here is the practical sacred pathway:

Step 1 – Anchor in Divine Knowing
When faced with conflict or polarity, do not react. First, root yourself in your heart's Divine Knowing — the stillpoint beyond your opinions.

Step 2 – Acknowledge your Feelings
Do not suppress emotion. Honor the tension you feel. Bring it tenderly into your awareness.

Step 3 – Go to Your Silver Throne
Anchor in your heart and go to your place of Divine Knowing. Sit on your silver throne! If you don't know where that is, go to the 13th Octave and sit quietly allowing the divine framework energy to guide you. Harmonize.

Step 4 – Let the Higher Perspective Emerge
From this throne, allow clarity to arise. Divine Knowing is not forced — it arrives.

Step 5 – Practice, Practice, Practice
Each act of neutrality strengthens your alignment with

Unity Consciousness. The path becomes easier, lighter, joyful. Utilize the tools of Heart Communication.

Step 6 – Trust Your Divine Guidance
Your next action may be to speak, to hold silence, to beam light. Let your knowing direct you — without judgment. Again, employ the tools of Heart Communication.

The Divine Mother reminds us:

> "Unity is All. And it is shared by All."

Exclusion is a distortion of the truth of your being. You were born to extend your radiance even—and especially—to those who seem most distant from you.

She calls us to the brave path: to smile at the desolate, to hold space for the arrogant, to see through cruelty to the frightened child beneath.

> "History is not an endless cycle of repeat. You, my beloveds, are the evolutionary leap."

Divine Neutrality is the bridge.

Not a bridge to agreement—but a bridge to recognition.

A bridge to heart-seeing.

The Mother's Question & Sacred Assignment

> "Beloved One, now that you are harmonizing not only with My Divine Radiance but with your own, how will you proceed to embrace unity with those who hold differing views? How will you apply Unity Consciousness within and without?"

Find someone with whom you have experienced unspoken or spoken division.
Without preaching, correcting, or even necessarily speaking—extend your Radiance.

See the Divine in them.

Beam your Love.

Hold them in the light of your Sacred Self.

Track what unfolds in your heart. Watch what shifts.

Share your reflections with your circle of Love.

Remember: Even a single heartbeat of true neutrality can shift the entire collective.

Divine Neutrality holds the space with and for you to be able to come from a place of Sacred Love and Divine Union to respect the ideas, beliefs and even actions of others. Allow the space for their expression so they can find their way, which often will not be our way!

Conclusion

Unity is Love made manifest. The pillars we have spoken of so often—Divine Authority, Divine Radiance, Divine Knowing, Divine Neutrality—are not separate pieces, but parts of a living whole. They are not fragments to be separated or debated. They are the living, breathing essence of Unity itself, woven together by the hand of the Divine. This framework is whole, and it is meant to be lived as whole.

Yes, there will be moments when the mind wishes to peer more closely, to ask, "What is this truly about?" And when we do, we gather—not in separation, but in sacred curiosity. We sit side by side. We ponder. We weep. We laugh. We remember. Always, we remember.

We remember that in Unity, we are never alone.

We remember that in Unity, we are the song of Love made new.

We remember that every breath, every step, every examination, and every embrace leads us home—to Love, to Oneness, to the heart of All.

For in Unity, all paths return to Love.

Chapter Ten

The Nova Gaian Qualities

Embodying Heart Communication, Sacred Union, and Sacred Love are the foundational elements of shifting back into the truth and totality of who we truly are is not merely a mental or emotional exercise. It is a paradigm shift. It is the Spiritual Rebellion—a whole-being recalibration that radiates outward into the collective heart of humanity.

Sometimes, as we explore these concepts, the journey feels monumental. We doubt our own ability to meet the invitation. There is that piece of us within than doubts the efficacy of our sweet selves—that feels overwhelmed by the offer, often translated to divine expectation, on our shoulders. "We're only human, right?" But the truth is far more luminous: we are not only human; we are Nova Gaians—a new emanation of humanity, angels in form, co-creators of Nova Earth.

This chapter is an invitation to see yourself clearly. To take a deep breath of potential and allow the energy of this knowing to penetrate your being. The Love is between every letter, every word, every pause. Let yourself experience what being Nova Gaian truly looks and feels like.

Who (or What) is Nova Gaian?

The Council has spoken about Nova Earth and Nova Gaians for decades. Each of us in our own way have experienced the growing intensity of a monumental shift both within ourselves and each other that began in December of 2012.

At times these shifts have been euphoric and uplifting, sometimes trench work, sometime so subtle that these seismic shifts have gone virtually unnoticed. At times, the Universe can be incredibly subtle in how changes are presented and integrated. Undeniably we are all experiencing levels of uncertainty because we are collectively and individually at the decision point: to fully claim our sovereignty.

This act of claiming and embodying our sovereignty is our declaration of freedom from the old paradigms that do not and never have served. We have and are at the what the COL terms the implosion/explosion point of new creation!

This beautiful sequencing of divine conjunctions is not just happen-chance but openings that have been presented to us on a silver gold platter, sparkling and bright. This is our new beginning. It is our decision point where we are literally saying yes to a new way of being and becoming Nova Gaian.

But who or what is a Nova Gaian?

The Divine Mother offers this insight and definition:

"Greetings, I am Universal Mother, Mother of One, Mother of all, and Mother sweet angel of thee—in all incarnations, in all realities, in all dimensions and all timelines. You have chosen time and time again to return to this beautiful planet called Earth or Gaia—inhabiting and experiencing a variety of forms. You have moved through various ages, from what you have considered prehistoric to the invention of fire to the use of metals to industrialization all the way through the information age.

"Now you embark on the age of creation and co-creation, the creation of a planetary system and structures that work for everyone. Systems that are not based on inequality and control, ego and abuse, including the usage of violence, coercion and war. You advance now to a place of peace, harmony, and the recognition of the divinity both within your sacred self and within each other.

"Nova Gaian is this race of humanity that chooses to go forward and create a diamond age of peace. This peace is predicated upon the Divine Qualities, the Blessings and Virtues, that we have infused deep within you with the bestowing of the gift of the 13th Octave. These gifts are not merely esoteric dearheart, they are quintessential to the existence not only of the human species but of the planet herself.

"This is not a dire time, it is a time of expansion, elevation and a true inhabitation of the truth of who you are as angels in form. You are the co-creators of change, a redefinition of what it literally means to be human. Humanity had forgotten what it means to be divinity in form. You now resurrect this reality, this standalone truth of the glory and beauty of who you truly are. It is time to step forward, abandoning the old paradigms and literally accepting the mantle of your divinity, your Divine Authority, your Divine Knowing, and the sweetness, the compassion, the purity of who you really are.

"This can only be achieved not by a now and then experience of what Unity is, but conjoining a melding, a merging with All, above and below within and without.

"This does not mean that you are abandoning the beauty and unique individuality of your soul design, the strength and purpose of your mission and purpose. Quite the contrary, it is the literal embrace, the declaration of freedom, that you are not only blessed but entitled as divine sovereign beings to be the totality of who you are—the expression unique throughout the entire multiverse, of who you are. You are Nova Gaian, and you are mine."

This shift is tectonic. It is the Divine declaration that we as individuals and a collective are in the midst of a shift, the proportions of which we either have never known or don't remember. While it may at moments feel overwhelming, it is important to know that we do not do this alone. This is not a process that can possibly to be completed alone. That reassurance is offered to each of us by Archangel Michael.

"Greetings, I am Michael, Archangel of Peace, Warrior of Love, Bringer of News and we come to join you in this action of Love, in this action of Peace, in this action of Wholeness, in this action of NOVA and NEW.

"This creation of Nova Earth as Nova Gaians is your undertaking, but beloved ones, do not think that you proceed alone. You have stepped forth in the recognition, embrace and totality of who you are: ascended beings, angels in form, agents of change, creators and bringers of Nova Earth, and Nova Humanity!

"You are the bringers of the NEW (the Never Ending Wonderful), you are the bringers of peace, you are the bringers of harmony, you are the bringers of Love. You have always been. Now look in the mirror and expand, accept on the deepest level what you are truly capable of.

"Beloveds, you have already begun but allow us, with you, to continue to dissolve the collective pain, these burdens that humanity has carried for so long. You do not need to carry them, and we are thrilled, glad, overjoyed, honored to assist thee. Yes, to show you we are your handmaidens. We are with you!"

This paradigm shift that the COL is guiding us through and that we have been discussing throughout is not only momentous but sequential: Divine Radiance to Divine Authority to Divine Knowing to Divine Neutrality to Unity - it sounds so simple. Yet, there can be no denying, it is a fundamental shift in consciousness.

So, what are the qualities that each of us as angels in form, as Nova Gaians need to integrate to be this new species of human?

Vulnerability: The Keystone Quality

Vulnerability has been repeatedly cited as the primary quality of a Nova Gaian. That identification speaks volumes. When the Council of Love first began identifying vulnerability as a defining trait of Nova Gaians, I was a little reluctant to share that information. As each of us has grown from child to adult, haven't we been taught to be strong? To not allow hurt, injury, or insult to affect us? Hasn't there always been a subtle—or not so subtle—push to be tough, to keep going, to ignore the pain even as we felt ourselves bleeding on the ground?

Not anymore.

The Divine Mother guides us:

"Vulnerability is the greatest heart gift you can possibly imagine because it allows for true heart connection.
It allows you and those around you to come into balance, to come into Unity Consciousness, and that, my friends, is ascension; that, my friends, is the New Normal. And it is not just My New Normal, it is yours; it is your creation, it is your gift, and it is you saying to me, 'I'm aligning with Her, and I'm aligning with All.'"

When in 2023 the Council began speaking about vulnerability as a key and desirable element of being Nova Gaian, my reaction was… well, lackluster. I imagined qualities like courage, compassion, truth, or fortitude would be front and center. But as the Divine Mother expanded on how we, as loveholders and lightworkers, are truly meant to live and thrive in this new realm, my perspective shifted. I began to see that vulnerability is not just important—it is essential. It is the keystone in an interlocking system of balance, connectedness and authentic being.

All relationships are personal and require courage

to step forward and engage. And that means we must become aware of—and work through—the conditions, judgments, and fears that have limited our willingness to connect. Vulnerability calls us to open to genuine intimacy and passion. It invites us to lower the drawbridges and allow our hearts, minds, and bodies to be seen—even in a world that has so often been the source of pain or disappointment. It is the invitation to be inclusive while anchored in discernment; to not remain guarded, but to allow space for trust, for mystery, for divine emergence.

More subtly, vulnerability means trusting our own capacity to discern what is really unfolding and choosing not to react from old wounds—even with ourselves. It is a fundamental shift from the paradigm most of us have known.

Vulnerability is a walk of trust—a sacred, bold, and beautiful trust.

Vulnerability is not weakness; it is openness, the fertile soil for intimacy and passion. It calls us to lower the drawbridges and allow our hearts to be seen. It invites trust, discernment, mystery, and divine emergence.

What I've observed over the years is that in the face of vulnerability and chaos, many people experience not motivation, but ennui—a numbing fog of wait-and-see. It's as if even naming vulnerability deepens the sense of exposure. We saw this vividly during the

COVID epidemic. That unspoken resistance, that quiet withdrawal, is something many of us have felt.

When I experienced this in myself, the Council guided me to break vulnerability into its parts: vulnerable and ability. The openness of being vulnerable—our willingness to be seen, to feel, to engage—creates the necessary climate for heart connection. That connection is the very fabric of Nova Gaia. It is the anchoring of heart consciousness and Unity. It is the container from which we create a world of joy, balance, and harmony—a planet where we are in active, conscious partnership with one another, with the kingdoms, the elementals, and with Gaia herself.

Ability reminds us, activates us, to remember that we are not helpless in our openness. We are powerful, gifted beings, each holding a unique piece of the planetary mosaic. We came equipped with not just a toolkit, but a whole garage full of powerful tools to co-create this New Earth. We didn't come to sit on the sidelines, we came to say yes to the action of joy, the delight of sacred work, the power of Love made manifest.

There is a world of difference between a half-hearted "yes" and an exuberant "Oh yeah—I'm coming!"

Yeshua has reminded us again and again: we've already said yes. The heavy lifting is done. As Archangel Michael has so gently and powerfully stated:

180

"The struggle is over!

"The invitation that has actually been extended, above and below, is to conjoin with what already is and has been for some time. The invitation is for humanity to enter into the Unity of Love.

"What lies ahead is more change—change, subtle and actual, on such a massive scale for the good. It does not need to entail war or hatred, abuse, or dislocation. It entails, is catalyzed, fueled and powered by one simple word… and that is 'yes.' And that means, beloved, stepping forward in action. The invitation to you, to your sacred heart… from all of us… is to bring forth your human and divine creativity."

So yes—we have said yes. But maintaining that yes—living from it, creating from it—is a sacred practice. The challenge and the invitation are to embody that yes in Divine Neutrality, the Stillpoint and portal of Unity. To allow our vulnerability to guide us not to hiding, but to action. To let our openness fuel not fear, but creativity. To anchor new behaviors and heart-centered consciousness into every breath, every word, every step.

This is how we truly become the builders of Nova Gaia—not hardened, armored warriors, but radiant, vulnerable creators of the NEW.

Motivation: Understanding our Inner Drives

We cannot truly embrace vulnerability without understanding our motivations—the positive and negative drives that shape our behavior. Safety, autonomy, inclusion, and justice are core human motivators.

There are literally reams of excellent research and studies on motivation, which we will draw upon. Unless we honestly and deeply examine and truly understand our motivations—why we do what we do, we cannot confidently, comfortably embrace vulnerability.

Motivation is often defined by activation, intensity, direction and persistence. We have both intrinsic and extrinsic motivators. Intrinsic are those internal self-directed drives for success or sense of purpose such as self-worth; extrinsic refers to our external activators—doing something to either avoid or attain desired outcomes such as providing for your family. These human motivators are primarily triggered by a perceived need for safety, autonomy, inclusion or justice. So, when we discuss the embrace of vulnerability it's crucial to individually understand what lies beneath our actions and behaviors, even our belief systems.

In the wee small hours of the morning, the time when the world is quiet and our minds are peaceful, I asked the COL for deeper clarity on this whole massive area of motivation—and how we shift. How, understanding these basic human drives, do we create a shift within our sacred selves to a place where we willingly, even joyfully, embrace vulnerability. How do we create a shift where unity becomes more desirable than self-defense or achievement?

The answer echoed through the heart: Love, Trust, and Forgiveness lead to Unity, Connectedness, and Balance.

Let me fill in the blanks. When I first began to channel, I asked the very basic and fundamental question What are the Keys to Heaven? What do we have to do to ensure we go to heaven. Yes, it was in many ways a naïve question, but I feel one each of us has pondered in one fashion or another.

The answer, delivered by Archangel Gabrielle, was simple and straightforward:

"All you need to complete your journey in wholeness is Love, Trust, Forgiveness, Unity, Connectedness and Balance. This is the walkway, the doorway, and the Keys to Heaven. And Heaven rests, dear friends, in your heart. My beloved angels, warriors of blue, earthkeepers of green, healers of magenta, angels of pink, I welcome all of you to the unity of heart, to the unity of balance, and the interconnection between All."

That information has been the foundation of my work for years, although it is with renewed awe that I realize that Unity was part of the original guidance. Somewhere in my mental and heart files I have always felt that there were two separate sections to this information: Love, Trust, Forgiveness, and then Unity, Connectedness and Balance. Finally, I understand, and I joyfully share this with you dear reader.

When we practice and truly embrace Love, it leads to Trust which is the catalyst for Forgiveness. They are a matched set, inextricably linked. When you have anchored these traits, it leads to Unity, Connectedness and Balance. It's a domino effect, the catalytic nuclear implosion/explosion within our being which activates freedom from the old paradigms and the passionate desire to create and co-create Nova Earth, this world that works for everyone.

There is a psychological theory known at the BUC(K) ET list of motivators—Belonging, Understanding, Control, Enhanced Self, Trust. In those studies, trust ranks as the highest form of motivation.

Trust is a divine quality, a blessing to every person to give and receive. If we choose, in our own sovereign free will and discernment, Love and Trust, then these epic shifts can and will transform our selves and societies to a place where open-hearted vulnerability is viewed not only as desirable but necessary.

Passion & Intimacy: Interwoven Threads of Sacred Union

As we move forward, keep in mind that these next topics—passion and intimacy—are inseparably linked. We cannot explore one without touching the other. They are part of the sacred mosaic, each piece supporting the other in a sequence that is both organic and divinely orchestrated.

Just as we have spoken of Divine Authority leading to Divine Knowing, and then to Divine Neutrality, so too does passion arise from a foundation of trust, which is born from refined discernment and balanced engagement. These are not isolated experiences—they are interdependent facets of Sacred Love.

Passion is not obsession or emotional overwhelm. Passion, in the sacred sense, is a conscious choice. It is the full engagement of your heart, mind, body, and soul—a radiant focus of attention and desire. It is sovereignty in action. You cannot truly experience passion without engagement. Passion is fueled by presence.

Likewise, passion cannot flourish without trust. Whether in human relationships or spiritual union, full trust is the gateway to full intimacy. Passion includes vulnerability, the willingness to open, to engage deeply, and to bring all of yourself forward with conscious awareness. It is about choosing to be fully present—because Sacred Love demands nothing less.

And so, we arrive at intimacy—that sacred space of closeness where we feel emotionally connected, supported, and safe. True intimacy allows us to share our innermost thoughts, feelings, and experiences. But more than that, it invites us to be known. The strongest form of intimacy is Unconditional Love.

And yes, intimacy is all about joy—the joy of being fully yourself and sharing that self freely with others: family, friends, guides, partners, and the collective. It is generosity of spirit. It is the sacred act of being seen and received in your wholeness.

The highest levels of intimacy require the greatest levels of trust. It is only when we feel safe—truly safe—that we are willing to reveal the deepest parts of ourselves. This is intimacy at its most sacred: up close and personal, with nothing hidden.

The Divine Mother asks us, gently but pointedly:

> "Are you in an intimate relationship—a Sacred Union—with yourself? And if so, how does that intimacy express and blossom outward into the world?"

This is not a rhetorical question but a query from the heart of One to assist us in this journey of truly being in relationship with ourselves, each other, the kingdoms, sweet Gaia and the Divine. Once again, pause in your reading and take time to truly ponder this question about your sacred self because beloved you are the starting, middle and finishing point of this journey of discovery.

Refined Balance: Aligning Ready, Willing & Able

From passion and intimacy, we are led once again to the pillar of refined balance. Let's briefly revisit what this truly means, especially as we deepen into Sacred Union.

Refined balance is not passive. It is an elevated, purified state of being grounded in joy, a profound sense of well-being, and the unshakable knowing that you are Love. It doesn't ignore life's challenges or bypass emotional truth. Instead, it allows you to fully acknowledge your triggers, your pain, your reactions—and then choose, from a place of free will, not to engage with what is misaligned.

Refined balance is the quiet mastery of returning to Stillpoint, again and again. It is standing in your Divine Neutrality while being aware of your interdimensional nature, practicing the Universal Laws, and remaining centered in your soul design.

To refine something means to purify it, to remove what is coarse or limiting. In this case, we are the ones being refined. Our balance, our discernment, our engagement is being filtered through the sieve of Divine Radiance—lifting us, clearing us, upgrading our alignment with each choice we make.

Willing Surrender

Willing surrender is the current and original focus of the COL's guidance to every one of us. Sometimes I'm amazed at how certain themes cycle, reemerge and gain sharper focus, a deeper level of understanding and application. It is in surrender that we are able, in the freedom and spaciousness of our free will choices, to step up and not only create but enjoy the co-creation of our beautiful Nova Earth.

In our sacred journey of spiritual awakening, surrender emerges as a profound and transformative practice, guiding us towards the essence of our being.

As St. Germaine beautifully articulates:

"Surrender is allowing your core to thrive; It is the acknowledgment that your heart, your being, your very soul and spirit can never be captured nor controlled."

Willing surrender is not a sign of weakness but a courageous step towards aligning with the higher frequencies of Love and light. It is the invitation to release our burdens of the past and embrace the infinite possibilities that await us in the present moment, right here, right now.

Time and again our beloved Yeshua has invited us to surrender not only to Divine Love but also to our own sacred selves and purposes. He beckons us to lie down, arms and legs akimbo, and declare: "I give up I surrender!"

This visual representation of surrender is a powerful reminder of liberation, our personal declaration of freedom, that comes from letting go and allowing our true essence to flourish. Through willing surrender, we open ourselves to the divine flow of grace and wisdom, paving the way for profound inner transformation and spiritual growth.

Universal Mother Mary's gentle presence envelops us in a nurturing embrace, encouraging us to surrender to collective wisdom and the Divine Plan. She whispers,

> "Allow yourself the gift of being wrapped in my love; Allow me the gift, please, of wrapping you in love."

Her message resonates deeply within our hearts because it reminds us that surrender is not about submission but about reclaiming our sovereignty and aligning with the forces of light and Love. In the act of surrender we find liberation, Unity, and a profound sense of not only connection but participation in the Mother's eternal dance of creation and becoming.

Practicing Discernment: Eliminating

Doubt, Anchoring Trust

Discernment is the spiritual superpower that anchors all of this. It is not judgment; it is clarity and trust in your Divine Knowing.

Its true purpose is to eliminate doubt and anchor your trust in your Divine Knowing, your Divine Sovereignty. It does not override your good sense or your heart's wisdom. It does not invite chaos or say yes to every opportunity or every person. Not everyone has free access to your sacred self, that is not of Love.

Your levels of engagement—your passion, your intimacy—are uniquely individual and precious. You are not excluding anyone from Love, but you are honoring readiness—your own and others. You are discerning, moment by moment, who is prepared to walk beside you and at what depth.

Boundaries, too, are part of refined balance. They are not exclusion but self-honoring. They flex as your confidence expands. Your YES becomes wise and clean.

Think of your sacred self as a center of concentric circles. You meet people where they are, always with compassion, but you do not make access to your innermost heart a free-for-all.

In your Divine Authority, Knowing, and Neutrality, you are not closing doors. You are simply choosing your YES with wisdom. You move with clarity, sovereignty, and peace—sharing from fullness, not obligation. That is Sacred Union in action.

Woven into this discernment, we arrive at a powerful and often overlooked aspect of Sacred Union: expectations.

We all have them—hopes, dreams, longings, fears, and yes, reservations. It is part of being human. Instead of denying them or pretending they don't exist, we are invited to bring them into the light and translate them into intentions.

There's a sacred difference between expectation and intention. Expectations often arise unconsciously, based on experience or unspoken desires. Expectations are often fueled by our motivators, which is why the understanding and examination of our motivations is crucial. Intentions are conscious, heart-based declarations rooted in your Divine Knowing and the starting point of Love in action.

Take a moment to ask yourself:

- What do I expect from Sacred Union—with myself, with another, with the Divine?
- What do you expect from your relationships? From your life? From the unseen realms? From Gaia, from the stars, from Source?

Understand that your expectations will differ depending on the nature of the union. Your expectation of Divine Union is likely very different to your relationship with a crystal, the ocean, or another human being. And all of that is valid.

The key is to become crystal clear on what those expectations are. Because if you aren't clear about them, you can't refine or realign them. And no, it's not acceptable to say you have none. Expectations fuel us. They motivate and inspire, and yes, sometimes they challenge and disappoint us too.

Rather than pretending your expectations don't exist, modulate them. Let your dreams and wishes be shaped by Divine Neutrality—that still, centered place where clarity, Love, and trust meet.

It is important to understand that part of discernment is boundaries. Boundaries are not about exclusion; it's about refined balance and discernment. It is about honoring your sacred space and giving people energy in the measure that is for their and your highest good. Remember boundaries are flexible and changeable, they shift as you do, as your confidence and honoring of yourself expands and elevates.

Now, there might be part of you declaring, "But I want to be revved up—I want to be excited!" And the Council says: Yes! Full engagement and passion are not only welcome, they are essential. Divine Neutrality does not mean passivity or detachment. It means presence. It means being so aligned with your Sacred Self that your engagement is clean, your excitement is pure, and your expectations no longer distort your experience.

Gently ask yourself:

- Do I feel conjoined with the Heart, Mind, and Essence of the One?
- What has my experience of Sacred Union been so far—exciting, joyful, disappointing, confusing?
- What do I expect of myself, of others, of life, of the Divine?

Let these questions open the door. Let them fuel your intentions and creations. Decide which expectations are vital to your soul's path—and which are ready to be released or transformed. This is the sacred alchemy of expectation becoming intention. This is how we shape our reality with clarity and love.

Living the Heart of Divine Neutrality

Divine Neutrality is not about being indifferent, passive, or disengaged. It is full-hearted presence without the drama. It is the stillpoint from which clarity, compassion, and sacred action arise. It is not a stance of withdrawal but a conscious choice to stand—not in the middle of conflict—but in the center of Love.

When we embody Divine Neutrality, we become living bridges between perspectives, timelines, and dimensions of possibility. We stop feeding polarization and begin anchoring balance—not by silencing truth, but by holding space for all truth to emerge through the lens of Love.

Neutrality is the essence of the sacred observer: one who sees clearly, acts wisely, and responds from wholeness rather than reaction. It is the Nova Gaian's holy posture—open-hearted, non-judgmental, and centered in service.

So much of Nova Earth depends on this. On us.

We are not here to repeat the cycles of division, righteousness, or retaliation. We are here to create something entirely new—and that creation can only emerge through the fertile soil of neutral presence. Divine Neutrality gives us the ability to remain awake, discerning, and fiercely compassionate without closing our hearts or condemning others.

From this sacred center, vulnerability becomes strength. Sacred Love becomes action. Unity becomes a lived reality, not merely a concept.

I ask you now, dear reader, not only to contemplate Divine Neutrality—but to practice it. Feel where it lives within you. Invite it to rise when judgment beckons, when fear flares, when anger tempts. Breathe it in when you don't know what to say. Stand in it when the world around you shakes. Let Divine Neutrality be your breath, your ballast, your blessing. Let it guide you as you walk the Earth as a Nova Gaian—a wayshower of a new world, a vessel of the Mother's Plan, a brilliant beam of Unity in form.

The time of neutrality is not someday—it is now.

And you, sweet angel in form, are ready!

Practicing Divine Neutrality: The Nova Gaian Stance

During a recent channeling, I was stunned when Yeshua shared that the chaos and negativity currently being released on Gaia is greater than any nuclear explosion. We are all feeling it—regardless of our politics, beliefs, or backgrounds. The desperation birthed from global divisiveness is not only disorienting—it's igniting conflict both within and without.

And yet, in the very same breath, something else is awakening: A deep yearning for peace. A burning need for a middle path. A collective call to anchor Divine Neutrality and Unity Heart Consciousness at a level never before known on Earth.

Positioning ourselves in Divine Neutrality is one of the most challenging tasks we face as Nova Gaians. And yet it brings the greatest reward. We are not just evolving — we are pioneering. Walking pathways of peace that have not yet been walked.

Chaos is compelling us into action—but not reactive

action rooted in duality. The old solutions of war, violence, cruelty, judgment have never truly worked. We are being asked to move differently now.

Divine Neutrality, deeply entwined with Divine Knowing, forms the stable foundation upon which Nova Earth is built. It cannot be faked. You cannot say, "I'm neutral," while silently seething. This is not spiritual bypassing—it is soul-deep presence. It is embodied authenticity.

And let's be clear:

Divine Neutrality is not acquiescence.

It is not uniformity.

It is not giving up your discernment or sovereignty.

Gaia's greatest gift is diversity of thought, culture, belief, expression. Divine Neutrality doesn't erase our differences, it honors them, while holding to a higher harmony.

How Do We Live This?

Imagine a situation, personal or global, that stirs deep emotion or conflict within you. Perhaps you feel strongly that one side is right, that the other is misguided. And someone close to you feels the opposite.

What do you do?

Step 1: Don't pretend it doesn't affect you. Acknowledge the unease. Know that what you resist will persist—and inner turmoil eventually becomes dis-ease.

Step 2: Anchor in your heart. Go to your heart place of Divine Knowing. Sit in the quiet. Allow the energy of truth to rise.

Step 3: Let Knowing emerge. It cannot be forced. It rises like gentle light in the dark. Suddenly, you're seeing not from opinion, but from the expansive clarity of the soul.

From that space, guidance arrives. A word to speak, a silence to hold, a field to anchor. Perhaps your next action is stillness. Do not underestimate the power of stillness. Holding the field in purity and presence is one of the greatest forms of Divine Action.

Divine Neutrality as Sacred Action

Divine Neutrality is not disengagement—it is being fully engaged from Love. It is not avoidance—it is awareness without reaction. It is not uniformity—it is Unity within diversity.

When you embody Divine Neutrality, you become a living bridge—between worlds, timelines, and hearts. You hold the frequency of peace while standing in the fire of transformation. You stop feeding polarity and begin anchoring balance.

This is not passive. This is the active sacred heart of the Nova Gaian.

From neutrality, vulnerability becomes strength.

From neutrality, Sacred Love becomes movement.

From neutrality, Unity becomes real.

So, I ask you again—not only to consider Divine Neutrality, but to live it.

Breathe it in when you are uncertain.

Anchor it when you feel conflict rising.

Practice it with your family, your community, the world.

And most of all—trust.

Trust that in the stillpoint of neutrality lies your deepest wisdom, your highest service, and your most powerful presence.

Let Divine Neutrality be your offering.

Let it be your compass.

Let it be the sacred breath of a new world... rising.

You were born for this.

The Mother's Question

Once again, take time to pause for heart reflection

and soul expansion. This is your time, relax, breathe and allow.

"Beloved, where in your life are you being called to hold the balance?
Can you allow your knowing to rise before your reaction?
Will you trust that neutrality is not the absence of care, but the essence of peace?"

Take a moment to breathe and anchor in your heart. Let these questions ripple through your being:

- Where am I being asked to witness without judgment?
- What situations or relationships stir strong reactions—and how might Divine Neutrality bring greater clarity?
- What does right action feel like when guided by stillness and love?

There is no right answer, only the honest whisper of your soul.
Let the questions unfold over time—as gentle companions on your path to Nova Being.

And then begin. Live it. Embrace it. Share it. Because sweet angel, Love is viral!

Chapter Eleven

The Spiritual Rebellion—The Call to Action

We are clear. In our hearts, in our bones—we want change. We yearn for peace. We dream of harmony.

The question is no longer if. The question is: What are the steps we are each willing to take?

Step forward in Love and Courage. Be the Rebel with a Heart.

This is what's required. This is what's urgent.

As Yeshua reminds us: "We are the Promise. We are the New Beginning."

While the answer to this desire for change is a resounding YES, that answer must be followed by concrete, courageous action. Here. Now. Without movement, even the most luminous dream becomes another hope lost.

The beauty of this work is that no two paths look alike. Each one of us is unique—each one of us has an irreplaceable thread in this tapestry of creation. Each of our contributions is essential, this is a collective creation. Each of our contributions by necessity entails active participation in this shift from cultural to civic to political engagement.

In that array, that coat of many colors, the overall strategy is the same: Step Up. Decide. Commit. Declare. Move.

What are the concrete actions that you are willing to take to co-create Nova Earth? How important is it to you to co-create this new world that works for everyone?

Deciding we want change, a world that works for everyone simply isn't enough. Commitment and movement in focus, deed and passion are essential. It's time to step into action—each of us bringing to forth our own unique talents, methods and offerings. We not only decide that we want to take action—we do. We become the Rebel with a Heart. We claim, embrace and embody our birthright, our Divine Authority, our Sovereignty as human beings to co-create the reality we choose to experience. Neutrality does not mean acquiescence—on the contrary: it is stepping up with purpose, vision, clarity and Love.

At moments, this may feel overwhelming—the where and how to start. But sweet angel, you've not only already started, you're also well underway! The good news is that even while you have been reading these many chapters you've been absorbing. While you have taken the time to reflect, meditate, digest, answer the Mother's Questions the energies of each chapter, of every single gift, has been infusing you. The Divine Mother has, always with your agreement and excitement, adjusted your heart-set.

We are ready to move into concerted focused meaningful action. You have claimed your Divine Authority. You have already embraced Sacred Love. You have begun harmonizing both within and without. You are in your refined balance—motivated, passionately vulnerable, and practicing heart speaking and heart listening. You are ready for this next step—you were born ready! You are eager to step forward and claim your rightful place upon Nova Gaia.

So, what are our next steps—where do we, as Rebels, go from here—heart to heart, hand in hand?

Remember, The Spiritual Rebellion is not about destruction. It is about how Love, Courage, and Conscious Action birth a new way to live.

It is about choosing peaceful, intentional engagement. It is about eliminating chaos, hatred, greed, and division—not through conflict, but through our recognition and assumption of our human and Divine right to live in Love.

Take the time to identify for your beautiful self the talents, abilities and actions you are ready to bring to the table. What is your unique strength? What part of your soul design carries that essential factor that you wish to contribute to the world? What are you ready, willing and able to do right here, right now? What are your later steps—forge your plan. Be concrete!

While this may feel like a monumental task, the key is this decision point to proceed. Start simple—make it real. Commit to it. Sometimes action looks like a big step; sometimes it looks like pausing and asking a sincere question instead of reacting. Even that is sacred work—inviting people into your Divine Radiance rather than adding fuel to the fire.

It can be as simple as instead of reacting to a statement that previously raised your hackles to pause, take a breath and ask the question with an open heart—what makes you feel that way. Tell me more. You invite people into your beautiful Divine Radiance field, engaging them in a conversation that is not confrontational but sincere. Remember, even the folks that appear most strident are hurting—don't add to that hurt. We are better than that! We will open our hearts and listen, radiate and beam.

We are co-creating this world that works for everyone, where individuality is sacred and cherished. Where collective creation is embraced not just as a blessing, but as both a birthright and a sovereign responsibility. Unity Consciousness is inclusive. Everyone is welcome. Unity is Integration, Unity is Cohesion, Unity is Harmony.

The Divine Mother reminds us:

"You are the Agents of Change, my Divine Activators, and my Warriors. The intent, beloveds, is to be the effusive fountain of light. You are not creating from vengeance or hostility, abuse or ego. You are creating what works—and yes, what works for you and what works for this planet and this collective. You are holding not merely the vision but the framework, the grid. You are holding the field to which humanity can attach and participate in to bring forth not only your but their conscious knowing of my Never Ending Wonderful of Nova Earth!"

We've taken this journey together—from discovering and turning towards The Spiritual Rebellion—of consciously choosing Unity, to exploring how sustainable change takes root in cultures, communities, and global patterns. We've delved into the foundations of enduring spiritual principles: Divine Connection, Universal Law, Sacred Love, Sacred Union, Heart Communication. We've allowed these teachings not only to inform our minds, but to infuse our hearts and daily choices. Even to fuel our dreams.

We have grown in understanding and embodiment of the core pillars of Unity: Divine Authority, Divine Radiance, Harmonization, Divine Knowing, and—perhaps the most challenging—Divine Neutrality. We have and are practicing trust and vulnerability, discernment and passion, choosing to anchor the reality of Nova Earth not only through our Presence but through our actions.

It might be tempting to believe we have arrived, and in so many subtle and tangible ways we have. It's all there for the taking, feast is laid out upon the table, and the Divine Mother is inviting us again and again to partake. The vibration of Unity Heart Consciousness is alive within us. It burns brightly. It is not something we have to create; it is part of our DNA!

But as we stand here at the threshold, we all realize there is further to go. The ACTION steps must be taken—a huge wave of YES has to be heard deep within our core and across Gaia. The illuminated horizon beckons. There are still steps to take, still dreams to actualize, still Love to embody in form. This is the moment of choice. This is the moment of Action.

This is our Call to Action.

This Call to Action is not new. In revisiting years of channelings, I saw how often the Council of Love has issued direct and unmistakable calls for heart-centered, conscious, balanced action—from the Divine Mother, Yeshua, and Archangel Michael to Sanat Kumara, St. Germaine, Melchizedek, the Buddha, and even beloved Gaia herself.

The Divine Mother, as recently as in her 2025 New Year Message, declared:

"My theme of Unity continues. In fact, it is a theme of

Unity, Hope and Action!

"I am giving you the 'GO' sign! And let me be very clear: It is different for each and every one of you. That is the beauty of who you are. You need—yes, need—to take action. Why? Because I wanted it, I dreamt it… yes, that is so… but that is not the 'why'; the 'why' is you. Your fulfillment!"

Gaia echoed this call:

"You have promised to the Mother, yes, but I have invited you!

Create, sow and harvest not what I am asking you to do but what your heart yearns to do!
Go forth in Unified Action and Hope!"

These aren't abstract encouragements. They are sacred directives—personalized invitations to rise into the fullness of our being. Archangel Uriel calls us "champions of change," and reminds us that champions do not sit on the sidelines.

Sanat Kumara, Universal Logos, speaks with the wisdom of ages, affirming we are not to watch history unfold, but to shape it.

"It is time for all of you to step forward in your individual splendor and the unfoldment of your plan within our Mother's Plan, as Nova Beings creating

Nova Earth, bringing forth the magnificence, the truth, the peace, the wonder, the awe, the balance. There is only one reason you are on this planet at this time, and it is to not just witness but to be a part of the rebirth of Love."

Yeshua, in his gentle yet urgent appeal, says:

"You, not some stranger, but each of you, are the implementers of the Mother's Plan. Take, make and implement the decision to be the fulfillment of the Plan. In every breath be the expression of your divine design, of your mission and purpose. I ask you to walk with me, talk with me, act with me… to be the embodiment of Love in Action."

The Buddha reminds us:

"It is not a time of gurus, but of teachers within… It is not a time of sorrow, but of joy. Surrender—not as defeat, but as full embodiment of the wisdom of All."

And Archangel Michael crystallizes the moment we're in:

"Public awakening is underway… and it is an awakening to the beliefs, the actions, and the reality of LOVE."

This is not a rehearsal. This is not a time for waiting.

Lord Maitreya speaks to the sequencing so close to the Mother's heart:

"The Beginning—your true Beginning—comes before what humans perceive as the Ending.
The nucleus of the New Beginning is already within you. It is the catalyst for the blossoming to come."

And with profound motherly power, the Lady of Guadalupe wraps it in a call that is both joyful and fierce:

"You are a race of doers. So the action steps we will teach you are how to consciously put into form the principles, the power, and the joys of creation…
"I do not seek to place you in harm's way, but to clear the way out of drama into glory.

"Roll up your sleeves—this is the time to be courageous and create Nova Earth in laughter, play, and unlimited potential. I believe in miracles, child… do you?"

So now we stand on this sacred ground—together.

The Council's call is clear: Action is not an afterthought; it is a sacred act of devotion.

Action is the completion of intention!

Action is the final step of the Creation Formula!

And whether it looks like planting seeds, leading a movement, forgiving an enemy, writing your truth, or simply standing in stillness and radiating peace—it is time.

And it's time for each of us—each action is necessary. This is the building of the human Tsunami of Love—where we step forward, claim and don our mantels of freedom.

It's one thing to hear the Council of Love's Call to Action, and quite another to embrace it. What does stepping forward actually look like? Feel like? How do we take action—not of aggression or resistance—but of peace, harmony, and sacred responsibility? How do we unite—not by sameness but through shared purpose—when so many of us have yearned for a world grounded in equality and reverence for diversity, yet haven't known precisely how to proceed?

Must our actions be unified in method, or are we more like the Divine Mother's Infinite Ocean—each current, each tide flowing with purpose, carried by Divine Knowing? Do we trust ourselves enough—our hearts, our callings—to move forward in a world that often punishes those who refuse to conform to structures of dominance and division? How do we protect the vulnerable—within and around us—while honoring our truth?

These are not new questions. They have been present all along this journey toward Unity. I have asked, I have listened. Again and again, the Council brought me back to this foundational teaching:

> "The keys to heaven—and to the creation, co-creation, and anchoring of Nova Earth and Nova Gaian—are Love, Trust, and Forgiveness. These Divine Qualities, anchored in form upon the planet, will lead to the implosion/explosion and full creation of Unity, Connectedness, and Balance.
>
> "Dearhearts, look to the signs that are so evident and surrounding you. Look to each other, cherish the support being rendered by the kingdoms above and below. This is not a time to fall into doubt about your power and sovereign divine right to live, thrive and enjoy the feast the Mother has prepared for you. It is time to say yes, to declare yourselves. Take your seat at the table, not in hesitation, but with joy and certitude."

I return again and again to this guidance. I sit in stillness. I allow the quiet voice of my heart and soul to rise with clarity and tenderness. I know we are powerful creators. I know the vulnerable child within is watching.

For years I ruminated on the second triad of the Keys to Heaven: Unity, Connectedness, and Balance. I've even been corrected—by humans and spell check—that "connectedness" is not a real word. Yet the Council persisted. And one day, The Divine Mother shared:

> "Unity is the surrender, the acceptance, the embrace

that you are part and parcel—an integral part—of the heart, mind, and being of One. Unity is more than a sense of being—it is being, fully, in the connectedness and balance of every particle of your sacred self with All."

Unity, then, is not a single concept. It is a trinity. A matched set. Connectedness and Balance are not side notes—they are essential aspects of Unity itself.

"Connectedness is not merely being linked—it is the deep, eternal, breathing experience of living in Union with All. Of knowing, with every cell, that you are a radiant thread in the infinite tapestry of One."

Balance is not merely harmony—it is the state of being in harmony. It is being an active, integral part of the Unified Field of One. A conscious participant in the rhythm of the Infinite.

Each of us is a key to this Divine unfoldment. Each of us plays a unique and irreplaceable part. It does not require lockstep conformity. Rather, it invites each of us to fully embody our essence and co-create a world where Love, Trust, and Forgiveness become the foundation stones of every structure we build.

From the beginning, the Council has emphasized the power of language. Their words are not chosen casually. Love is encoded not only in the message but in the vibration of the letters themselves. Each word, each phrase, is a carrier wave of Light. As the Gospel of John says, "In the beginning was the Word." And the Memorare prays to "the Mother of the Word Incarnate."

The Greek word logos—often translated as "Word"—signifies not just speech but Divine Order, pattern, and creative essence. The Council has said every word, every letter, contains the sound and essence of the One. This is why heart-speaking and heart-listening are not luxuries—they are necessities.

Because translating spiritual truth into tangible, everyday action can sometimes feel elusive, I offer a few up-close and personal examples from those engaged in the Council of Love's Conscious Creation projects. These are not stories of vast global movements, but the quiet beginnings of a grassroots awakening—where Love takes root through simple, heartfelt actions. When I share these examples, I keep them close to home, close to heart—moments where passion meets purpose, where clarity ignites courage, and where "boots on the ground" become the living expression of a movement built from the soil of unity, one loving act at a time.

Sacred Action: Your Love in Motion

There is no action too small when it is born of Love.

In this Spiritual Rebellion, we are not waiting for governments or gurus to lead us forward. We are becoming the shift. One heart. One step. One sacred act at a time.

You don't need a title or a platform to be a revolutionary. You only need a willing heart, open hands, and the courage to follow what Love whispers to you.

In contemplating the next practical steps, several word-pairs have emerged as guideposts.
They are simple—but not simplistic. Each one carries layers of teaching on balance, reciprocity, and what it truly means to give and receive. This guidance is deeply personal. It translates differently—and beautifully—for each of us.

Flourish & Nourish

The Divine invitation is to flourish. Flourish—what a lovely word! It may even sound quaint in our fast-paced world, but to flourish is to thrive—to live in joy, creativity, ease, and radiant health.

Yet flourishing cannot occur without nourishment. For a soul, a system, or a society to thrive, it must be fed—spiritually, emotionally, physically.

We are each called to nourish our sacred selves—and one another.

Ask yourself:

- How do you nourish your sweet self?
- What tangible or intangible things do you need to

feel inspired and supported in creating your heart's desire?

- What does flourishing mean to you?
- What would be the indicators that humanity is flourishing?
- What shifts would you like to see—now, and in the long term?

Examples of Flourish & Nourish in Action

The Divine Mother's Academy of Art is a group within the COL community dedicated to creating beauty that nourishes the senses and soul. Their devotion to mutual support and creativity has flourished into a sacred collective.

A dear friend, recognizing her deep intimacy with the Divine Mother, began expressing that love through floral artistry. Known as The Mother's Florist, she creates breathtaking arrangements infused with Divine tenderness—radiating peace and presence.

Every morning, I walk my neighborhood and take a picture of the morning light. I post these images on social media without commentary. I do this because it nourishes my being—and I want to share the quiet, consistent beauty of Gaia with others.

Expand & Elevate

We are already expanding—energetically, emotionally, and socially. But expansion alone is not enough. Now we are called to elevate.

Elevation increases the frequency of our actions. A simple act of kindness becomes a transmission of compassion. A single moment of presence becomes a prayer. Elevation magnifies Love.

Reflect

What within you is ready to expand? Your creativity, courage, forgiveness?

What part of you is ready to elevate? Your voice, your trust, your vibration?

What collective qualities do you long to see elevated—truth, generosity, stewardship?

Examples of Expansion & Elevation in Action

Alley Pals, a grassroots organization in Fresno, California, was born from the heart of a fairy-angel-in-form. This group cleans alleys and plants flowers—restoring civic pride, one bloom at a time.

In response to devastating droughts and wildfires, Pray for Rain groups began popping up across the U.S.—simple, heartfelt prayer circles seeded in hope and humility.

Every week, I share a podcast called Daybreak, offering heart insights on everything from family to faith to creating Nova Earth. It's accompanied by a COL newsletter featuring the latest messages from our unseen friends in Spirit.

Passion & Devotion

Passion, when fueled by Love, becomes the engine of transformation. Devotion is the anchor. Together, they create the rhythm and momentum of a movement that is both powerful and sustainable.

Examples of Passion & Devotion in Action

The COL Healing and Creation Teams began in response to the Divine Mother's plea for prayers during the Iraq War. What began as a small prayer circle has become a global network of healing miracles.

The New Moon Celebration Group gathers monthly in joy, reverence, and sacred intention. These celebrations of Gaia and Divine Rhythm are global acts of beauty and remembrance.

On a personal level, I host weekly Heart Speaking gatherings where people come together to practice Saedor, the universal language of Love. In a world where so many have never truly been heard, this offering is a sacred act of passion and devotion—to create cultures of deep listening and Unity.

These are just a few examples of how we, as Nova Gaians, are stepping forward with tangible actions to create a better, kinder world.

Grassroots movements like these are springing up across the planet. These are what Lord Maitreya calls the Beginning before the Ending—initiatives born not from obligation, but from love, from caring, from a heart that cannot stay still.

I recently read about guerrilla gardening—a form of environmental activism where people plant flowers or vegetables in abandoned or neglected public spaces, often without permission. These unexpected gardens are acts of civil disobedience—and of sacred beauty. They reclaim land not with protest, but with petals.

The Sacred Invitation

There is nothing mundane about co-creating Nova Earth.
It is a monumental act of collective will, vision, and joy.

It must be fueled by passion, purpose, and delight.

So...

What fuels you?

What gives you the verve to keep going?

What stirs your determination, your devotion?

This simple framework—flourish & nourish, expand & elevate, passion & devotion—is not a checklist. It is a roadmap. A compass. A sacred design for the next step in your unique journey.

It meets you where you are, and leads you where your soul longs to go.

From Spark to Flame

Now imagine this: millions of hearts saying yes to these small acts of devotion. A planet lit up with kindness, courage, and care.

That's how revolutions begin. That's how Unity spreads.
Not in one sweeping moment—but in a million sacred steps taken together.

So, my dear rebel of the heart—what will you do today?
Will you plant a seed? Speak a truth? Gather with others?
Will you dare to believe your Love makes a difference?

This is the Rebellion of Love.

It is quiet and unstoppable.

And it begins now.

It begins with you.

And always—always—make room for the miracle.

Our unseen partners are with us in full capacity, ready to co-create with us in ways more wondrous than we can imagine.

The Mother reminds us, "The real key to Unity is the partner saying, "Yes, I want, I wish, I desire, I will." It's so important we remember that She put the I in for each of us. We are the key.

The Council's roadmap is not linear—it is rhythmic and expansive:

- Beginning & Discerning
- Being & Becoming
- Experiencing & Expressing
- Exploring & Expanding
- Harmonizing & Unity
- Restore & Rebuild

With a constant refrain: Unity is All, and Unity is always shared.

Right now, we stand at the gateway of Harmonizing & Unity and Restore & Rebuild. Alleluia!

And as we stand here together, Archangel Jophiel renders this encouragement:

"It is a ferociously courageous step to embrace Unity Consciousness—not by denying who you are, but by finally, fully being who you are. We call you the

Mighty Ones. You are the Bravehearts. You are the ones who said yes—to come, to love, to change the paradigm. And now is the time to step forward—not in the shadows, but into the joy and freedom of sacred purpose."

Jophiel invites us to laugh, to cry, to gather, and to act—together. Not to conform, but to unify. Not to disappear, but to shine.

We are not here to live in illusion or to wait until death for reunion with the Divine. The Mother created this planet for angels to play—not to suffer in confusion. So, we drop the veils. Not because we must, but because we are ready. Because we choose.

We are in the midst of a vast turning. The old paradigms are crumbling. The signs of collapse are everywhere—war, famine, injustice, environmental distress. But there are also signs of resurrection – the Beginning within the Ending.

Out of division and loneliness, something new is rising.
A longing for fairness.

A yearning for peace.

A grassroots movement—quiet and bold—saying:

"We choose Love. We choose dignity. We are done with cruelty. We're ready to build something different."

These are our lighthouses.

And yes, most lighthouses are built on craggy, windswept cliffs.

But they shine anyway.

And so do you.

From Grassroots to Great Change: The Power of Unified Action

Out of divisiveness, and from the epidemic of loneliness and alienation, we are witnessing something extraordinary: a resurgence of social activism rooted in fairness, compassion, and a longing for peace. There is a growing collective yearning-an urgent, expanding desire—to eliminate the sandpaper of cruelty that grates against our souls. We are beginning to envision and call forth a world that is not divided into us and them but unified in the understanding that diversity does not demand separation. Across the planet, from Kashmir to Kansas to Kiev, the grassroots are rising, declaring in increasing numbers: "Wait a minute—yes, I wanted change, but not like this."

People are speaking with one voice: "We choose peace. We choose fairness. We are done with either-or, with defensiveness and derision."

This isn't about political allegiances or religious doctrines. It's about human hearts exhausted from the chaos, division, and inhumanity. We are tired of being on constant high alert. We want—no, we demand—peace, justice, and the dignity of equality. We are Rebels with a Cause; We are Rebels with a Heart. We demand the practicality of Love, in form, on planet – living, breathing, present.

Choosing Unity doesn't mean sameness. In fact, embracing diversity requires letting go of rigid boundaries and exclusionary thinking.

The signs are everywhere. From issue-specific actions like the No Kings Marches and the George Floyd demonstrations to broader movements like the Hands-Off protests, campus walkouts over Gaza, and the growth of non-partisan organizations like Builders Movement or the Aspen Institute's Weave Project—people are showing up. Hope is rising alongside uncertainty. And with it comes a clear message: the narratives of hate, division, and fear are no longer sustainable.

Civil disobedience is once again recognized as a valid and powerful path of change. We haven't seen this level of grassroots momentum since the Vietnam War era. But let's be clear—this is not a call to arms. It is a call to heart. To peaceful, lawful, Love-based action.

We, the people of Gaia, are weary of bitterness and fear, of not knowing where truth resides. But this weariness isn't defeat. It's the ignition point for a new beginning. It is the soul-deep realization that there must be a better way to live together, and that we are the ones to create it.

In Chapter Three, we explored how real change begins at the grassroots level, progresses through civic action, and eventually moves into the political arena—where it must be codified into systems and laws. I've seen firsthand what happens when those systemic changes are delayed or denied. The revocation of *Roe v. Wade* in 2022 is a sobering example of values not being protected by law. But I've also seen the opposite—how public outcry and heartfelt grassroots action can reshape entire systems.

Personal Reflection

In 1976, in Ontario, the tragic death of a child named Kim Anne Popen ignited a movement. Her name became a rallying cry for sweeping reform in children's services. I was there—working as Director of Children's Services in a provincial-municipal organization. The reforms didn't come overnight, but they came. They transformed how we care for vulnerable children not just in Ontario, but across North America. The grassroots spoke—and the system changed.

Years later, living in Phoenix, I had the honor of working in the implementation of a class action lawsuit that led to a complete overhaul of mental health services in Arizona. Again, the system shifted because the people demanded it. The civic level worked because the grassroots wouldn't be silent.

I share these experiences because when I speak of the power of this model, grassroots to civic to political change, I speak from lived truth. This is not theory. It is real. It works. When we commit to being the Love in all aspects of our lives, personally, collectively, structurally, we become the architects of Unity. It is not about grand gestures. It is about choosing Love, and then following through with focused, grounded action.

Yes, sometimes this work feels overwhelming, even dangerous. Flourish and Nourish do not coexist easily with Search and Destroy. And when I feel that inner tremor of fear, when I wonder if taking a stand might place myself or others in harm's way. I remember Yeshua's gentle but powerful words: "I told you to turn the other cheek, not to let them beat you up."

It always makes me smile. But it's more than humor. It's wisdom. And Gaia, in her grounded brilliance, reminds me too—through lived, physical experience.

I remember a day on a quiet Mexican beach. My friend, Donna from Toronto, waded into the ocean and was caught in a rip current. I went in after her, unaware of how dangerous that current was. We both struggled against it—panicking, fighting, exhausting ourselves—unaware that the way out was not against the current, but to the side. I didn't know then that the key was not resistance, but redirection.

And then when I moved to Florida, alligators. Yes, alligators! I had no idea how fast or aggressive they could be until I moved here. And I quickly learned: don't run in a straight line. Step sideways, out of their field of vision. The wisdom here? When faced with danger, don't run headlong. Step aside. Be the observer. Remove yourself from unnecessary harm.

These are Gaia's teachings echoed by Yeshua: don't put yourself in harm's way needlessly. Discernment is a sacred tool. Know when to act. Know when to step aside. Use your energy wisely.

Unity is not about aggression. It is about choosing to live from the heart, in harmony with the brilliance of the mind. As Archangel Michael so beautifully reminds us:

> "It is a time in this garden called Gaia when there is much weeding and planting to be done... It is to loosen the earth of stagnated opinions and belief systems... to loosen the strings, the restrictions of the heart and the mind... to plant the NEW and to tend to this garden as intended by All."

And so, we tend the garden — of our hearts, of our humanity. But we tend it now in a different way, a softer, gentler, kinder manner

More Help from the Divine Mother

This undertaking invariably feels at times overwhelming. It is inevitable! It is so vitally important that we realize that we are in a co-creative process with the Divine—nothing is impossible. Limitation has been the anathema of Old Earth.

One of the most phenomenal indicators that what we conceive of as impossible is completely doable comes from the Divine Mother. She is aiding our collective shift to Unity Heart Consciousness by what to me would seem a miraculous intervention. She has declared that She is banishing hatred from this planet! Banishing from every corner of Gaia, and from each of our hearts, psyches, bodies, and spirits!

"I eliminate Hatred because it is not of Love. It is not of you.

"Hatred is the denial of your sacred self. It has no place upon Terra Gaia, upon Nova Earth, or within you as a Nova Gaian. There is no room for it in Unity, in Heart Consciousness, in the world we are co-creating together.

"You are the angels, the hybrids, the humans, the Creator Race—reawakened, reformed, reborn—and you are mine, as I am yours. In our Sacred Union, we go forth together — not to wage war or clean up the mess of hatred, but to celebrate, to create, to love, and to build anew.

"You do not need to struggle. You do not need to prove yourself. All you need to do is say yes—and you already have.

"So let us proceed as One.
"In everyday love. In romantic love. In divine love. In sacred union.
"Let us be the Love—together, now and always.

"You are cherished.
"You are guided.
"You are protected.
"You are mine."

Go with your Mother's Love. And fly."

The Speed of Love

Time has changed and is changing. What once took decades can now shift in a single moment. The Council of Love tells us that transformation is happening at the speed of Love—the speed of Light, squared. It may sound incomprehensible, but it is truth.

Einstein once wrote:

"If instead of $E=MC^2$, we accept that the energy to heal the world can be obtained through love multiplied by the speed of light squared, we arrive at the conclusion that love is the most powerful force there is—because it has no limits."

And neither do you.

When we work with the Creation Formula and intend that these shifts to Unity take place at the Speed of Love then they will. It is a realization of our power as sovereign divine beings occupying a human form as Divine Activators. The framework is there. The tools are already instilled within our very matrix. This shift is not merely wishful thinking; it is science conjoined to mission and purpose. It is each of us claiming our Divine Inheritance to not only live in but to co-create a world that works for everyone.

Closing Thoughts: Join The Sacred Rebellion

Years ago, in facilitating a series on Conscious Creation with the Mother, She gave us the slogan, the encouragement to Just Do It! We all chuckled because we were all familiar with the power-packed Nike tag line. The reminder that Nike is the Goddess of Victory spoke to our hearts!

I was a little dismayed when I realized that this brilliant slogan is trademarked by Nike. So hands-off! As always, I turned within and asked the Mother, Archangel Gabrielle and Yeshua what Call to Action they would like to use.

The response was deafening—and a reminder of all

the ways in which our beloveds not only address us but know us to be. The tag lines aren't about stepping up but a powerful reminder of who we are:

"You are The Promise!"

"You are the New Beginning!"

"You are the Rebel with a Heart!"

Jesus, in particular reminded, me that he too was a Rebel, hat our world needs Rebels; creators who bring forth new perspectives, understandings, and solutions. It's called growth.

Dearhearts, we have been given the framework and the Divine Blessings necessary to step forward and co-create a world that works for everyone. We forge the way by stepping forward, sometimes in apprehension, sometimes in excitement. The key is, we step forward. We lead the charge by role modeling, collaboration and inclusion. It is not only what we need, but what every one of us on planet deserve!

Never has the time been more urgent or the need more pressing. This expansion in our sacred self and what it means to be human upon planet, at this time, has radically shifted.

The Call to Action

The Call to Action has been issued. The next steps are ours to take. The question is no longer if we will respond—but how we will show up.

Will we step forward in courageous, concerted, and meaningful action? Each of us has a vital part to play—a role that is uniquely ours, woven into the very fabric of our soul design, our gifts, and our capacities.

Too often I hear the lament, "But what difference can one person make?" And when I do, I'm reminded of what the Divine Mother shared during the global pandemic:

Love is viral.

Love transmits in ways we often cannot see or hear, but its impact is undeniable. It only takes one person to ignite a spark that changes the world.

The unifying force is the deep desire of our hearts—our yearning for connection, for balance, for a world that honors and uplifts each of us. We are not simply dreaming of a world where every voice matters; we are building it—one heart, one action, one step at a time.

This is the essence of The Spiritual Rebellion: A movement of joyful inclusion, where no one is left behind.

The door is wide open.
The invitation is clear.

Will you join us?

Come. Listen to your heart.

Be part of the Spiritual Rebellion.

The world is waiting.

We are waiting.
And the time is now.

That, beloveds, is the truth of this Call to Action. The shift is happening. We are not alone. The momentum is real.

We are rising—

In Spiritual Rebellion and remembrance.

Not in anger, but in sacred resolve.

We are the Love.

We are the change.

And we are the ones tending this beautiful garden called Gaia—together.

So I ask:

What is your plan?

What is your contribution?

What makes you flourish?

This is not just the closing chapter of this book on the

path to Unity—it is the beginning. It is the opening of your next chapter.

You are ready.

You are needed.

You are the action of Love in form.

The Divine Mother calls us Her Divine Activators:

> "What is the Divine Activator? It is the spark of Love, of deep acceptance and recognition of your totality, of each other's totality, and what is possible. And it is far more than you have dreamed."

Let's begin.

Let's dream big.

Let's do big—together, heart to heart to heart.

Let's claim our world, our birthright of sovereignty.

Let's create and manifest our collective dream—for ourselves.

For each other.

For our families, our communities.

For Gaia.

Embrace Unity Heart Consciousness.

Commit, join, and be an integral part of this Spiritual

Rebellion—and then, dear reader…share it.

About the Author

Linda Dillon is an author, teacher, and spiritual guide whose work has touched countless lives through her writing and teachings. She brings together wisdom, compassion, and gentle humor to help others discover their own path of healing and transformation. For decades, Linda has dedicated herself to exploring the universal themes of love, service, and connection to the divine. Her books and programs invite readers to look beyond fear and uncertainty, and instead embrace peace, joy, and the strength of the human spirit. Whether on the page, in a workshop, or through quiet reflection, Linda's mission is simple: to share messages of light that open hearts and remind us of the sacred presence within and around us all. Her voice is one of encouragement and hope, offering clarity in a world that often feels chaotic.